Bobby Owsinski's

DECONSTRUCTED HITS
MODERN ROCK & COUNTRY

Bobby Owsinski's
DECONSTRUCTED HITS
MODERN ROCK & COUNTRY

**Uncover the stories & techniques
behind 20 iconic songs**

Alfred Music
LEARN · TEACH · PLAY

LOS ANGELES

Alfred Music
P.O. Box 10003
Van Nuys, CA 91410-0003
alfred.com

Produced in association with Lawson Music Media, Inc.
Library of Congress Control Number: 2013951016

ISBN-10: 0-7390-7342-7
ISBN-13: 978-0-7390-7342-1

Cover illustration: record: © Dreamstime.com / Aureiko

Alfred Cares. Contents printed on 100% recycled paper.

Contents

The Hits

PREFACE

Of all the regular posts on my Big Picture music production blog (bobbyowsinski.blogspot.com), the most popular are always the ones involving the analysis of hit songs.

I first started doing these analyses after finding a few isolated tracks from various hits (which almost everyone loves to hear) on YouTube and providing some commentary on them. Slowly that turned into a much deeper analysis, similar to those I've included in a couple of my books to illustrate how an arrangement in a hit song actually works. Eventually I expanded on that idea to encompass a lot more than the arrangement, and that's what you'll read here. Now, each song analysis looks at the song itself (its form and lyrics), the arrangement, the sound, and its production, as well as some key song facts and trivia.

While you're reading these analyses, try listening to each song, and I guarantee you'll begin to hear it differently than ever before. You'll find yourself listening *through* the song instead of to it. Rather than the wash of a complete mix, you'll begin to hear all of the individual parts of the arrangement, the production tricks, and the audio intricacies. Most of all, my aim is to identify and highlight the tangible reasons for why the song was not only a hit, but also an enduring one. Every hit has an intangible factor to it that can't be described, but there's a lot under the hood that absolutely can.

I hope you'll enjoy reading these song analyses as much as I did making them. They are a great learning tool for any engineer, producer, songwriter, or musician, as they really do help you to look deep inside the actual workings of a hit. If you're just a fan, you'll enjoy them too, because you'll listen to some of your favorite songs in a completely new and different way.

How to Listen

Since you're reading a book about listening to music (actually *through* the music), it's helpful to have a few pointers on what to listen for. Here I break it down to a general listening technique and then add an additional advanced listening technique for musicians and engineers, who probably already have more refined listening skills. If you aren't familiar with a term, check out its meaning in the glossary at the end of the book.

General Listening Technique

While this might seem like a long list, these are just some of the things that an experienced studio ear will hear almost automatically. You can train yourself to do the same pretty easily. Just start with a few at a time, and before you know it, you'll naturally be listening *through* the song, instead of just hearing it. Beware that after listening like this, you can sometimes get too analytical and lose the enjoyment of the song for a while (it happens to most first-year college music and audio students).

- **Listen for the instruments that are providing the pulse to the song.** All music, even dreamlike ambient music, has a pulse, and that's the first thing you want to notice.

- **Listen to the ambience.** Does a vocal or an instrument sound like it's in the room right in front of you, or in a club, a church, or a cave? Is there an audible reverb tail? Can you hear it repeat after it stops playing?

- **Listen to the clarity of the mix.** Can you hear each instrument and vocal clearly in the mix? Are some buried so you can't distinguish what they are? Can you identify all the instruments that you're hearing?

- **Listen to the clarity of each instrument or vocal.** Does it sound lifelike or distorted? Is there an effect used to alter its sound?

- **Try to identify each section of the song.** Is something new happening the second and third time you hear a section? Is there a new vocal or instrument introduced? Is one taken away? Is an effect added or subtracted?

- **Try to identify the loudest thing in the mix.** Is the vocal louder than the other instruments or is it lower than the rest of the band? Is the bass out in front of the drums?

- **Identify the hook of the song.** What instrument or vocal plays it? When does it occur? Is it built around a lyric? Does it even have one?

- **Listen to the stereo soundfield of the song.** Are there instruments or vocals that only appear on one side? Are there instruments that appear on both sides?

- **Listen to the overall timbre of the song.** Does it seem bright? Too much bass? Is there an instrument or vocal that stands out because of its timbre?

- **Listen to the dynamics of the song.** Does it breath volume-wise with the song's pulse? Does it sound lifeless or do the instruments and vocals sound natural like you'd hear in a club?

- **Is the song fun to listen to?** Why? Why not?

ADVANCED LISTENING TECHNIQUE

The following guidelines are for those readers who have some musical or studio knowledge, who may want to listen with a bit more precision.

- **Listen for the time signature.** Where's the downbeat and how many beats until the next one?

- **Listen for the number of different sections in the song.** Do the sections repeat? Does the song have a bridge? Is there an interlude between sections?

- **Listen for the number of bars in each section.** How long is each section? Is it the same length the next time it repeats? Are there any extra bars of music? All music isn't symmetrical in that it won't necessarily have 4-, 8-, 12-, or 16-bar sections, and in many cases you'll find an extra bar before or after a section.

- **Listen to the chord pattern(s) of the song.** Does it change from the verse to the chorus or bridge? Does it change the next time the section repeats? Is there a key change in the song?

- **Listen to the song's melody.** Are there big jumps, and if so, in what section are they?

- **Listen for any delays on individual instruments.** Is the delay timed to the track so the repeats are in sync with the pulse of the song? Is the same delay used on multiple instruments or are there different ones?

- **Listen to the ambience of the song.** Is there more than one environment? Does each one have the same decay? Does each one have the same timbre?

- **Listen for the compression in the song.** Can you identify which instruments are compressed? Can you hear the compressor working? Does the song sound more or less compressed than other songs you're familiar with?

- **Are there any doubled instruments or vocals?** Are they panned in stereo?

There are a number of other listening details besides these, but these are good starting points. Of course, the song analysis will point most of them out with more precision as you read and listen along. Happy listening!

CHARACTERISTICS OF THE AVERAGE HIT SONG

Here are some interesting characteristics common to hit songs including those in this book. You won't find them all in every song, but the majority of hit songs exhibit at least some of these traits.

- **Most hit songs have a short intro.** It's always been about getting to the point, and that never seems to change.

- **The melody in the chorus tends to be higher in pitch than the verses.** This builds intensity and energy as the song progresses.

- **The chorus and the bridge have more intensity than the verse.** This is due to either more instruments or vocals entering, or greater performance intensity from the players.

- **The song's intensity builds from beginning to end.** Most songs start off less intense, and then gradually grow with each section. It then peaks towards the end of the song, either on the bridge or the outro choruses.

- **The ending can date a song.** Songs before 2000 tended to use fade endings, but more recent songs tend to use a hard ending. Hard endings are said to play better in the digital world, where a fade is more likely to make the listener skip on to the next song.

As you go through the songs in the book you'll see a number of similarities in song form, arrangement, and production. That will be a great help if you're a songwriter, arranger, or producer. The more you know about how hits are made, the more likely you'll actually have one.

Keep in mind that even though you may not like a song or an artist, it's still worth checking out the song analysis. Hits are hits for a reason, and they are definitely hard to come by. Every song included here has some sort of magic as well as some common elements, so something can be learned from every single one.

THE FIVE ELEMENTS OF A GREAT ARRANGEMENT

Before we look at the first song, here's an overview of the five elements of a great arrangement, which is something you'll see in every song analysis.

Most well-conceived arrangements are limited in the number of arrangement elements that occur at the same time. An element can be a single instrument such as a lead guitar or a vocal, or it can be a group of instruments such as the bass and drums, a doubled guitar line, a group of backing vocals, and so on. Generally, a group of instruments playing exactly the same rhythm is considered an element. Examples include a doubled lead guitar or doubled vocal, both single elements even though there are two of them; also a lead vocal with two additional harmonies. Two lead guitars playing different parts can be two elements, however. A lead and a rhythm guitar can be two separate elements as well.

The five main arrangement elements are:

- **The Foundation (the rhythm section):** The foundation is usually the bass and drums, but can also include a rhythm guitar and/or keyboards if they're playing the same rhythmic figure as the rhythm section. Occasionally, as in the case of power trios, the foundation element will only consist of drums since the bass will usually have to play a different rhythm figure to fill out the sound, so it becomes its own element.

- **The Pad:** A pad is a long sustaining note or chord. In the days before synthesizers, a Hammond Organ provided the best pad and was joined later by the Fender Rhodes. Synthesizers now provide the majority of pads but real strings or a guitar power chord can also suffice.

- **The Rhythm:** Rhythm is any instrument that plays counter to the foundation element. This can be a double-time shaker or tambourine, a rhythm guitar strumming on the backbeat, or congas playing a Latin feel. The rhythm element is used to add motion and excitement to the track.

- **The Lead:** A lead vocal, lead instrument, or solo.

- **The Fills:** Fills generally occur in the spaces between lead lines, or they can be signature hook lines. You can think of a fill element as an answer to the lead.

Most arrangements have these five elements, but very rarely are they all present at the same time. Sometimes as few as three occur simultaneously, but any more than five elements at the same time is confusing to the listener, and usually causes listener fatigue as a result.

Take note that none of the hit songs in this book have more than five elements happening at once, which is your first lesson in creating a hit.

The Hit Song Secret

A movie director once told me, "If you can get the viewer to laugh just once and cry just once in a movie, you'll have a hit." It seems like there's an analogy to that in the record business as well, as indicated 20 years ago by British psychologist John Sloboda and verified in 2007 by John Guhn of the University of British Columbia.

Sloboda conducted an experiment in which he asked listeners to identify passages in a song that register a strong emotion such as tears or goose bumps. The listeners found 20 such passages which Sloboda then analyzed; he found that 18 contained a writing device known as *appoggiatura*. An appoggiatura can be a passing note that clashes with the melody just enough to create a temporary dissonance, an entrance of a new voice, or song dynamics, all of which create tension for the listener.

All art is based around tension and release. In painting, it's black against white. In photography, it's light against the shadows. In music, it's dissonance against harmony or quiet against loud. Tension and release makes things interesting. You can't have any kind of art without it.

When several appoggiaturas happen close to one another in a melody, it develops a constant state of tension and release, which makes the melody of a song more powerful and provokes an even stronger reaction from the listener.

It turns out that there is actually a formula for appoggiatura that's comprised of four elements:

- Passages that go from quiet to loud
- An entrance of a new instrument or harmony
- A melody that suddenly expands its range
- Unexpected deviations of melody or harmony

All of these are great songwriting and arrangement devices that I'll point out in the upcoming song analyses. The fact that there have been actual studies that verify what we intuitively know shows that there may be some validity to the fact that there's a sort of formula to making hits, even though it's usually not something the songwriter consciously thinks about. One thing's for sure: surprises in volume level, melody, and harmony are what makes a listener's spine tingle. The next time you listen to a song, be on the lookout for one.

U2

Beautiful Day

Song Facts

Album: *All That You Can't Leave Behind*
Writers: Bono, Adam Clayton, The Edge, Larry Mullen, Jr.
Producers: Daniel Lanois, Brian Eno, Steve Lillywhite
Studio: HQ Studio (Dublin, Ireland)
Release Date: October 9, 2000
Length: 4:06
Sales: 500,000+ (single), 12+ million (album) worldwide
Highest Chart Position: #21 U.S. *Billboard* Hot 100, #1 U.K. Singles Chart

"Beautiful Day," the lead single from U2's 2000 album *All That You Can't Leave Behind,* was a huge commercial success and one of the group's biggest hits ever. The song won three Grammy awards for Song of the Year, Record of the Year, and Best Performance by a Duo or Group with Vocal. It hit #1 in many parts of the world, despite only making it to #21 on the U.S. *Billboard* Hot 100 chart. *Rolling Stone* magazine has rated the song #345 of its 500 Greatest Songs of All Time, while VH1 rates it at #15 on its list of the 100 Greatest Songs of the '00s.

"Beautiful Day" originated as a standard rock tune called "Always," but after Bono wrote the lyrics, the track took a different direction. The song had a long period of development as the band argued over The Edge's guitar tone—some within the group wanted the vintage U2 sound of their earlier albums and others did not. The mixing also took longer than usual as the arrangement was tweaked; Bono added a guitar track, a keyboard part was changed to guitar, and the bass line was modified in the chorus.

THE SONG

"Beautiful Day" is like many U2 songs in that it doesn't follow what might be considered a standard song form. It has two bridges, and, at times, the melody and arrangement of the chorus are altered to where it almost seems like another section. The song form looks like this:

intro | verse | chorus | verse | chorus | bridge 1 | intro |
bridge 2 | chorus | bridge 1 | chorus/solo | intro

The lyrics to "Beautiful Day" seem rather forced. There's no specific instance of the dreaded "moon-June" rhyming scheme, but it's close. The cadence is also strained; at times, Bono seems to have a mouthful of words that are difficult to sing in the course of a phrase. The melodies in the chorus and bridge are strong, as is the hook of the song, and these more successful elements make up for the weaker lyrics of the verses.

The BPM of the song is 136.

THE ARRANGEMENT

This is one of the few songs in which all five arrangement elements (and sometimes more) occur simultaneously. There are many different sounds that sneak in and out of the verses, but the chorus and bridges are about as dense as can be.

The song starts with a keyboard pad, electric piano and bass outlining the chords, and what sounds like a drum machine kick drum. When the vocal enters after 4 bars, so does a snare drum, doubled by a tambourine. After 4 more bars, a guitar enters on the right channel and a keyboard pedal note on the left. On the last 2 bars of the verse, a background vocal with heavy reverb enters on the right.

For the chorus, the band cranks up the vocal. The drums enter in full, with a guitar playing power chords on the left and the same background vocal with heavy reverb on the right.

In the second verse, the bass begins to drive the beat by playing eighth notes, and various guitar fills on the right and keyboard fills on the left drift in and out of the mix. During the second chorus, a new background vocal comes in on the right channel, this time lower in pitch and drier, making it more up front.

The same primary instrumentation continues during bridge 1, only with drummer Larry Mullen Jr. switching his snare pattern to the toms. The song then drops in intensity to another 4-bar intro, this time with a modulated guitar on the left—and then it's into bridge 2.

In the first half of bridge 2, the intensity lowers, with no drums, a keyboard pad, the bass playing whole notes, and the guitar playing an arpeggio. The drums return for the second half, building toward the chorus; but it's unusual in that it's 4 bars of background vocals accompanied by string and keyboard pads.

Then we're back to bridge 1 for a second time, with exactly the same instrumentation as the first. From there, it goes back into a chorus; but this time, only the first line is sung and a guitar solo enters on the right. The outro breaks down to just a tremolo guitar on the left and feedback that pans from left to right.

Arrangement Elements
The Foundation: Bass, drums, drum machine kick, tambourine doubling the snare
The Rhythm: The Edge's signature arpeggiated guitar
The Pad: Various synthesizers
The Lead: Lead vocal
The Fills: Background vocals, various keyboards and guitars

THE SOUND

The mix for "Beautiful Day" is dense, with many different synth and guitar sounds appearing briefly and then disappearing, some never to be heard again. It features depths of sonic layering using both reverb and delay. The Edge has always been a master of the delay effect on his guitars, but "Beautiful Day" features lush reverb on synths and background vocals as well.

One of the cooler elements of the mix is the panning. The keyboards lean left and most of the guitars lean right, except for the power chords in the choruses, the arpeggios in the second bridge, and the vibrato effect at the very end, which are all panned left. The background vocals are always on the right side (most unusually), and while The Edge's high vocal is bathed in reverb, Bono's low vocal is drier and more up front.

The drums are very small and tinny sounding (especially the snare), possibly because that was the only way to fit everything together in such a dense mix. On the verses, the snare is also doubled by the tambourine, making it sound thinner than it really is.

Bono's vocals are dry, which keeps them in the foreground of the mix.

Even though there are times during the song when more than five elements are occurring, the mix makes it all work. As new elements are introduced, the older ones are pulled back in level, allowing everything to work together effectively.

◀))) **Listen Up**

To the background vocals that always appear in the right channel.

To the second, lower background vocal that appears in the second and subsequent choruses.

To the feedback panning from left to right and back at the very end of the song.

To the various keyboard and guitar fills in the left channel during the verses.

THE PRODUCTION

"Beautiful Day" has all the hallmarks of a song where overdub after overdub was tried in an effort to come up with something that worked; and when it came to the mixing, they decided to use pieces of everything. That's the production trick here, where so many different tracks blend together without clashing.

That said, one of the best aspects of this recording is the dynamics. While many records build momentum and create dynamic tension and release by introducing new elements to the mix and then pulling them out, "Beautiful Day" relies on the skill of the band to go from a whisper to a roar. U2 has never been afraid to play quietly, and when you hear the transition from the first verse to the first chorus, you understand how valuable an asset that is. Since its release, "Beautiful Day" has been one of the band's concert staples, and it's easy to see why.

Foo Fighters
Best of You

SONG FACTS

Album: *In Your Honor*

Writers: Dave Grohl, Taylor Hawkins, Nate Mendel, Chris Shiflett

Producers: Nick Raskulinecz, Foo Fighters

Studio: Studio 606 (Northridge, CA)

Release Date: May 30, 2005

Length: 4:16

Sales: 1+ million (single)

Highest Chart Position: #18 U.S. *Billboard* Hot 100, #1 U.S. *Billboard* Hot Mainstream Rock Tracks, #4 U.K. Singles Chart

Together for nearly 20 years, Foo Fighters have had a lot of hits, but "Best of You" is the only one to go platinum, with sales of over a million units. The first single from their *In Your Honor* double LP, the song topped the *Billboard* Hot Mainstream Rock Tracks chart for four weeks, won the *Kerrang!* award for Best Single, and was nominated for a Grammy award for Best Rock Song.

Although credited to all four members of Foo Fighters, the song was written by singer/guitarist Dave Grohl while he was supporting John Kerry for president in 2004. Similar to what has happened with so many other hits by various artists through the years, Grohl didn't think "Best of You" was worthy of being included on the album, but he was persuaded by his manager to put it on. "Best of You" was also covered by the artist Prince during his 2007 Super Bowl halftime appearance.

THE SONG

"Best of You" is typical Foo Fighters, meaning it's quirky in many ways. Each verse and chorus change in length and feel, which is unusual for any song. For instance, a verse can be 12, 16, or 24 bars long, while a chorus may be 12 or 16 bars in length. The bridge is also odd in that it's a combination of guitar solo, change of feel, and verse. The form looks like this:

verse (12 bars) | chorus (12 bars) | verse (24 bars) | chorus (16 bars) | bridge/solo (16 bars) | chorus (16 bars) | verse (16 bars) | chorus (16 bars) | outro (8 bars)

The song is built around the same general chord pattern that's repeated in various combinations in different sections of the song except for the outro, which is a series of accents on the same chord as it builds to a crescendo.

The song's melody is strong, although it doesn't change much from verse to chorus. The lyrics are well crafted in that they read and sing well, tell a story, and even rhyme well.

The BPM of the song is 128.

THE ARRANGEMENT

"Best of You" begins, unusually, on a verse with no intro whatsoever, with just the vocal and a guitar playing clean sixteenth notes (another Foo Fighters technique). At bar 9, a second clean guitar is added on the right side, doubling the first; and then, at the beginning of the chorus, a clean guitar playing an ascending line is added on the right side. Once again, at bar 9 of the chorus, the bass is added as well.

On the downbeat of the second verse, the drums enter, and guitars switch from clean to dirty as the intensity increases by several notches. The snare and bass guitar play the same feel, while the drums play eighth notes on the kick, with a cymbal crash every other bar. At bar 9, a harmony vocal is added on what almost might be considered a B section. At the chorus, the drums begin to play the snare on every beat, with a crash cymbal every bar; and the ascending guitar line from the first chorus enters again, but this time, it's more distorted.

At the bridge, the feel of the drums changes once again, with the playing being more free and including a lot of tom fills and cymbal crashes. There's also a written guitar solo, and on the chord change at bar 9, the vocals enter, followed by full-band accents.

The next chorus begins with different lyrics for 8 bars and is followed by the main chorus lyrics for another 8. The bass doubles the ascending line of the left chorus guitar. On the next verse, the intensity is brought down to what it was on the intro, with the guitars playing a soft, clean, picking part against the lone vocal. At bar 9, the full band enters with yet another eighth-note feel and a full-band stop on the downbeat of the last bar. For the last chorus, the drums return to the same quarter-note snare feel as the second chorus, while the bass again plays an ascending line. The outro is a series of high-energy accents on one chord, and the intensity builds at the end with a guitar playing a bend in a high octave.

Arrangement Elements
The Foundation: Bass and drums
The Rhythm: Rhythm guitars
The Pad: None
The Lead: Lead vocals
The Fills: None (although the ascending line in the chorus could serve that function)

THE SOUND

"Best of You" is the typical Foo Fighters wall of sound: a sonic blitz from the time the entire band enters in the second verse. The mix is very compressed, especially singer Dave Grohl's doubled vocals, where you can hear the attack of the compressor grabbing onto some words, especially in the intro.

The mix features some nice panning to keep multiple guitars out of each other's way. The main rhythm guitar sits slightly left of center and is doubled by another rhythm guitar that enters on the right. To balance out the panning, a third guitar plays an ascending line on the left.

The drums sound pretty good, but the kick is somewhat low in the mix when compared to other rock songs. Also, the drums are almost in mono, with the cymbals panned only slightly to the left and right. The cymbals are mixed well; they're played a lot in the choruses but never seem to take up a lot of sonic space like in many rock mixes.

◀))) **Listen Up**
To the big breath on the vocal at the beginning of the song.
To the guitars spread left to right in the soundfield.
To the different drum feels in each section.
To the compression on the vocal in the first verse.

THE PRODUCTION

Foo Fighters are known for their intensity in concert, and they're one of the few bands able to capture it on record as well. That's partially due to the performances and partially because of their use of dynamics; in this song, they go from quiet to loud to quiet and end with a fury of intensity.

On "Best of You," the production shows its sophistication by taking a song that's basically built over the same repeating chord pattern and keeping it interesting. This is accomplished not only through the dynamics mentioned above, but also through the changes in feel between the sections, as well as the stops and accents, that make each section feel unique.

While you'd probably never call any member of the Foos a particularly great player, with the exception perhaps of drummer Taylor Hawkins, the intensity of the band overcomes musicianship every time. Capturing that is the essence of production.

Mutemath

Blood Pressure

Song Facts

Album: *Odd Soul*

Writer: Paul Meany, Darren King, Roy Mitchell-Cardenas, Todd Gummerman

Producer: Mutemath

Studio: Paul Meany's house (New Orleans)

Release Date: August 8, 2011

Length: 3:04

Highest Chart Position: #28 U.S. Billboard Alternative chart

Mutemath is part of a new breed of rock bands that isn't afraid to stretch the limits of what we're used to hearing. The song "Blood Pressure" off their album *Odd Soul* isn't what could be classified as a "hit," but sure is interesting, and the official video for the song is one of the most innovative music videos you'll ever see. Actually, *Odd Soul* debuted at #24 on the *Billboard* 200 chart, and "Blood Pressure" received significant exposure on VH1, eventually reaching #28 on the Alternative Songs chart.

The Song

"Blood Pressure" uses a fairly standard song form with some subtle tricks. The form looks like this:

intro | verse | chorus | verse | chorus | bridge | chorus | chorus | end

What's interesting is that the chord changes are a little different on the second verse and on the outchorus, and this keeps the song interesting. This is another song with a well-defined ending.

As for the lyrics, finally, here's a writer than can tell a story, make it work with the song, and be a bit clever about it at the same time. Not an easy task for sure, but that's part of the craft of songwriting.

The BPM of the song is 150.

THE ARRANGEMENT

The best part about "Blood Pressure" is that it seems like very simple rock, but there are a lot of additional parts that you only hear if you listen hard. All of the synth noises, extra guitar parts, and vocals that fill in the spaces between the vocals keep things interesting. As the song progresses, so do the extra fill parts (they're mostly on the right channel).

Arrangement Elements
The Foundation: Bass, drums
The Rhythm: Repeating guitar line
The Pad: No true pad in this song although you might classify the vocal harmonies at the end of the verses as a pad
The Lead: Lead vocal
The Fills: Various synths, vocals, guitars, noises

THE SOUND

Whoever mixed this song did a great job of effects layering. The drums and main guitar riff are fairly dry and in your face (there might be a very short room effect on both), the lead vocal octaves have a slight short hall or plate reverb, and the background harmonies have a very long and deep hall reverb. As a result, there's a lot of front to back action that puts all the instruments on an aural soundstage where you can almost see in your mind where the players are standing.

The panning is also very cool with the main guitar riff on the left channel and the fills on the right for balance, as well as a very wide drum track.

All of the tracks are fairly clean and distinct and nothing seems over-compressed, a sign of good engineering.

◀))) **Listen Up**

To the guitar panned far left and the fills panned far right during the verses.

To the piano that enters on the right during the second verse.

To the wide panning on the dry drums, making them sound like you're standing right in front of them.

THE PRODUCTION

There's a lot to like about this production. First of all the drums are very active in a Keith Moon sort of way, only a lot more controlled. The lead vocals doubled in octaves makes the song memorable, as does as the vocal harmony cluster at the end of each verse. The guitar chords are doubled in the chorus to make them seem bigger, a standard trick that works particularly well here.

Another thing to listen for is all the little noises and fills that increase as the song progresses, as well as the wah-wah keyboard in the second verse on the right channel.

Mumford & Sons

The Cave

SONG FACTS

Album: *Sigh No More*
Writer: Marcus Mumford
Producer: Markus Dravs
Studio: Rhubarb Studio (London)
Release Date: February 26, 2010
Length: 3:38
Sales: 1+ million
Highest Chart Position: #2 U.S. Billboard Rock Songs

Mumford & Sons' "The Cave" hit #1 on the iTunes Alternative Songs chart, and is the third single from the album *Sigh No More*, which won a Brit award for Best British Album of 2011. "The Cave" went on to sell more than a million copies, and was nominated for four Grammy awards, including Song of the Year.

The album *Sigh No More* went on to sell over a million units in the U.K. and over two million in the US. It was also the third most downloaded album in the U.S. in 2011 with over 750,000. The album then went on to place #1 on six separate *Billboard* charts, and go to #1 in the U.K., Australia, Canada, Ireland and New Zealand.

"The Cave" also found a life on television, figuring prominently in the *2010 World Cup* coverage, in Fox's *Lone Star*, and the British TV series *Skins*.

THE SONG

"The Cave" is typical of most folk songs in that it's just a verse and chorus form. The form looks like this:

intro | verse | chorus | interlude | verse | chorus | verse | chorus | chorus | chorus | chorus

The lyrics borrow from ancient literature, with references to Homer's *The Odyssey* and Plato's *The Republic*. They're very well woven together and stand as poetry if read alone. These boys can think.

The BPM of the song is 142.

THE ARRANGEMENT

This song is the one of the best examples of dynamics that you'll hear on record today. Listen to how the song breathes in volume from the quiet intro to the roar of the chorus, then back again. Then in the outro choruses, the first one is quiet, and each one builds to a climax at the end. It's proof that even a fairly simple song form in any genre of music can be made interesting with merely the addition of dynamics.

The song begins with the lead vocal and fingerpicked guitar, but on bar 9 the bass and a electric banjo (playing harmonics) enter outlining the chord pattern. On the first part of the chorus, the song again returns to just the lead vocal but now the guitar begins to play a quarter note chord rhythm pattern. As in the previous section, halfway through the chorus, the bass and piano enter as vocal harmonies join the lead vocal.

On the interlude, the band turns it loose with the banjo and kick drum entering as the piano plays a quarter note pattern and the guitar plays 16th notes strums.

For the second verse, both the guitar and bass play quarter notes as the piano plays whole notes against them, but on the second half, the banjo reenters and the guitar returns to playing 16th strums while the kick drum plays louder in the mix.

On the second chorus, the band continues playing with the same instrumentation but adds vocal harmonies on the first half as well as the second.

On the first half of the third verse, the intensity drops again as the guitar returns to playing just quarter note muted chord strums and the bass plays very quiet quarter notes. The song then goes directly into the chorus, where the bass drops out and a new arpeggiated piano line and a horn section enter. On the second half, the bass enters playing quarter notes and the harmonies join the lead vocal.

The band then plays another chorus with the same intensity and instrumentation as the second, only without the vocals, and with an "ah" pad part added. On the last chorus, the vocals reenter, but this time the lead vocal changes to high-register ad libs to increase the intensity. The song then ends on a hard ending on the downbeat of what would be another verse.

Arrangement Elements

The Foundation: Hard guitar strumming, bass, simple foot stomps (no drums except a kick drum, which is not only unusual, but amazingly well implemented)

The Rhythm: Electric banjo picking in the chorus

The Pad: Accordion, violin-like sound in the chorus

The Lead: Lead vocal

The Fills: Banjo and piano in the verse, recorder-like sound in the last chorus

THE SOUND

The mix is a bit muddy and it's sometimes difficult to pick out some of the instruments in the chorus, although this could have been intentional. All the instruments sound natural without a trace of over-compression. There's also a very nice short reverb with a timed short pre-delay on the vocal and other instruments that just about disappear into the track.

◀))) **Listen Up**
To the electric banjo harmonics in the first and third verses.
To the short room reverb on the vocal.

THE PRODUCTION

Any time you get this level of dynamics from a group of players, you have a tremendous performance since it takes a great deal of concentration to do it both smoothly and in sync with the other musicians. Of course, it's just this characteristic that makes Mumford & Sons who they are.

Once again, sometimes the best thing a producer can do is to leave things as they are and resist the temptation to add additional parts. "The Cave" is a great example of just that.

Coldplay

Clocks

SONG FACTS

Album: *A Rush of Blood to the Head*

Writers: Guy Berryman, Jonny Buckland, Will Champion, Chris Martin

Producer: Ken Nelson, Coldplay

Studios: Mayfair Studios (London), AIR Studios (London), Parr Street Recording Studios (London)

Release Date: December 10, 2002

Length: 5:07 (album), 4:10 (single edit)

Sales: 500,000+ (single), 13+ million (album)

Highest Chart Position: #29 U.S. *Billboard* Hot 100, #9 U.K. Singles Chart

One of the most successful songs of Coldplay's career, "Clocks" won a Grammy award in 2004 for Record of the Year and has been used in commercials, movies, and numerous song samples since. The track is from the band's second album, *A Rush of Blood to the Head*, which went on to sell more than 13 million units worldwide.

"Clocks" was written during the later stages of making the album, and it was nearly left off of it since the band already had enough songs. When the time came to deliver the album, the group felt it was still incomplete, so they revisited the demos put aside for their third album, and Coldplay's manager urged them to finish "Clocks." Since the album was running behind its planned release date, the song was recorded and mixed more quickly than usual, but it still turned out spectacularly well.

THE SONG

"Clocks" is another song with a standard form that's cleverly crafted into something very interesting. The form looks like this:

intro | verse | chorus (8 bars) | interlude | verse | chorus (16 bars) | interlude/chorus | bridge | intro | interlude/chorus | outro | ending

The lyrics are pretty abstract and don't connect as a story, much less a cohesive idea. They work in the context of the song, however, and are fairly well written. The second verse looks a little clunky to read but actually sings well, which proves that rhythmic cadence isn't always necessary for lyrics to work. It should be noted that the only time the song's title is mentioned is during the second verse.

The melody of the verse is catchy and memorable, although, unlike most hit songs, the chorus's melody is not. There's a great hook, however, and it's the piano part on the intro and choruses.

TheBPM of the song is 132.

THE ARRANGEMENT

If you were to look at the form of "Clocks" on paper, you'd think there was nothing special, but like many popular songs, the arrangement cleverly takes it to a new place.

The song begins with the signature piano line backed up by a dark synth pad. Halfway through the intro, the bass guitar, drums, and a higher synth pad enter—the drums playing an unusual beat that mimics the rhythm of the piano line. Both the bass guitar and kick drum play eighth notes but accent the piano line as well.

On the verse, the vocal enters, and the high synth pad and piano both exit. On the chorus, the piano enters again, as well as a guitar playing the rhythm of the piano line on the lower strings. The chorus continues for 8 bars, and then returns to the second half of the intro, with the high synth entering and the drums using more cymbals to raise the energy.

The second verse returns to the instrumentation of the first verse, except that halfway through, a harmony vocal enters and the synth pad plays a higher chord inversion instead of the descending pattern from before. The second chorus is twice as long, with the same instrumentation except for a harmony vocal entering on the second half. The song proceeds to an interlude section similar to the second half of the intro, but the piano line is cleverly played up a 3rd to distinguish it from previous sections. For the second half of the interlude, chorus vocals are added.

The bridge is more of the same instrumentation and rhythm, with a different melody and chord pattern, and a low vocal harmony. The guitar is more prominent, playing a pedal note and then trading eighth notes with the synth at the end.

The song is then broken down to just the piano line and synth pad for 8 bars, as in the beginning. Then it goes back into the previous interlude/chorus, with the vocals entering halfway through. The instruments continue as an outro for another 16 bars with a different melody and different lyrics, but the chorus vocals reenter halfway through. The song concludes with a slow fade in which the music breaks down to the higher piano line from the interlude, the lower synth pad, an organ bass, and a new guitar line.

Once again, the song seems simple on a quick listen, but even though there aren't many instrument layers or overdubs, there's a lot going on beneath the surface.

Arrangement Elements
The Foundation: Bass guitar and kick (unlike most songs)
The Rhythm: Drums (unlike most songs)
The Pad: Synth pad that enters with the piano in the intro and plays throughout the song, and a second synth that enters only on the choruses
The Lead: Piano in the intro and chorus, vocal in the verses (though it's almost secondary in the chorus)
The Fills: Guitar lines in the bridge and outro chorus

THE SOUND

"Clocks" is a good example of a style of mixing that's typically British in that it uses a lot of different sonic layers. Although most instruments have some reverb on them, the amount varies, with the synthesizer pads getting a deep wash that gives the song its sonic signature. The piano has what sounds like the same reverb, but less of it so it comes forward in the mix. The reverb decay is fairly long, and the high and low frequencies are filtered so it blends into the track well while being less noticeable.

The vocal is natural sounding and up front but sometimes lapses into sibilance. It has its own separate reverb that's timed to the track. The drums, which are somewhat low in the mix, are fairly dry and very present with a great cymbal sound. The bass has a lot of high end so it can be heard above the low synth pad and hold down the pulse of the song.

The panning is interesting. While the synths and piano are in stereo, the low synth leans to the right, while the piano is sometimes on the right and sometimes slightly to the left. The guitar, normally slightly to the left, is slightly to the right at the end of the bridge and then pans back and forth during the ending.

◀))) **Listen Up**

To the panning of the synthesizers and piano.

To the clock that sounds when "clocks" is mentioned in the second verse.

To the background harmony vocal panned slightly right.

To the guitar panning back and forth on the ending.

THE PRODUCTION

Although vocalist/keyboardist Chris Martin sells the vocal very well, Gerry Berryman takes a potentially boring eighth-note pedal part on the bass, plays it dynamically, and brings it to some unexpected places to keep things interesting. That's what's cool about this song; it's dynamic like most hits, but the number of sonic layers gives it a sound unlike anything on the market during this time period.

As with most hits with a simple song form, it's the little things that make the difference—like the piano line played up a 3rd during the interludes, the harmony vocals entering on the second half of the verse, and the subtle guitar parts that push the choruses and bridge along. There's more going on here than meets the ear.

Linkin Park

In the End

SONG FACTS

Album: *Hybrid Theory*
Writer: Linkin Park
Producer: Don Gilmore
Studios: NRG Recording Studios (North Hollywood, CA),
Soundtrack Group (New York City)
Release Date: November 21, 2001
Length: 3:36
Sales: 500,000+ (single), 24+ million worldwide (album)
Highest Chart Position: #2 U.S. *Billboard* Hot 100, #8 U.K. Singles Chart

"In the End" is the fourth single from Linkin Park's 2001 debut album, *Hybrid Theory*, and it was released a full nine months after the album release. The song became the band's highest-charting song ever in the United States and went on to have great worldwide success, as did the album. "In the End" is also *Billboard*'s second most played song of the decade and is somewhat timeless when it comes to iTunes, as it is still in the Top 10 on iTunes' Alternative Chart more than 10 years after its initial release. The video also has more than 100 million views on YouTube.

THE SONG

The form for "In The End" is fairly straightforward. It looks like this:

intro | verse | chorus | verse | chorus | verse/bridge | chorus | outro

The third verse varies from the others, being a sung melody instead of a rap, so it could be considered a bridge; and the chord changes are the same as the other verses until the second half, when they change to the chord pattern used in the chorus.

The strongest part of the song is its powerful melody and hook at the chorus. The lyrics describe broken trust and relationships, which proved extremely relevant to the band's audience. Also, the lyrics have a good cadence that doesn't feel forced, with a rhyming scheme that's strictly followed but works well within the context of the song.

The BPM of the song is 105.

THE ARRANGEMENT

"In the End" is a great example of dynamics, as, with every section, it breathes in terms of volume. It goes from a quiet intro to a louder verse to a huge chorus to a quieter verse, etc. It's very effective, and is one of the techniques that makes a song with this kind of form successful.

The intro consists of a stereo piano and rhythmic noise. This leads into the first verse, which is much larger sounding, thanks to the entrance of a low piano, bass, and drums. Also contributing to the bigger sound of the verse is a doubled melody vocal at the beginning of each 4 bars, the rap, synth lead, and a stereo rap double. On the second half of the verse, the piano from the intro returns.

On the chorus, the melody vocal takes over as the lead element, and doubled power-chord guitars panned left and right take over as the pad. The synth continues as a counterpoint to the vocal but is set very low in the mix.

On the second verse, the instrumentation remains the same, but the bass and drums accent beats 3 and 4 of the last part of the first half. The second chorus remains the same as the first.

In the third verse, the synth and low-piano pad drop out and the single-track vocal melody takes over. In the second half of the verse, there's a 2-beat rest underneath the vocal, and then the doubled guitars enter, playing the chorus's chord pattern without the synth.

The third chorus is, again, identical to the previous two. On the outro, the piano line continues, first with the same rhythmic noise as in the intro, and later with panned guitar feedback over the final piano arpeggio.

Arrangement Elements

The Foundation: Mostly the drums, since the kick sound buries the bass guitar and it's not very easy to pick out the notes

The Rhythm: Piano during the verse

The Pad: A high, single-note synthesizer line and low piano during the verse; doubled guitar playing power chords in the chorus

The Lead: Vocal—rap and sung melody

The Fills: Single-note synth line in the chorus; rap fills in the verses, panned hard left and hard right

---

THE SOUND

The sound of "In the End" isn't exactly what you'd call pristine, but then again, that's not necessarily expected in the genre of alternative music. The entire song is extremely compressed and, as a result, exhibits a fair amount of distortion. The mix is also a little muddy, with the kick drum so big it mostly covers the bass guitar and renders it difficult to hear distinctly.

You can hear the compression on the lead vocal in places, but the sound works in context. It's bathed in a rather long reverb that blends into the track so it's hardly detectable. The vocal is doubled everywhere except for the third verse/bridge, where it's just a single-track vocal, which makes it sound smaller at the appropriate time and different from the other vocal parts in the song. The vocal is placed low in the mix to make the band sound bigger, a common technique in rock mixing. The rap is dry and up front; it is doubled effectively at the end of each stanza, with one track panned hard left and the other, right.

The piano that's so prominent in the song is recorded in stereo, which spreads it nicely and leaves space for both the melody vocal and rap. During the chorus, the doubled power-chord guitars are split left and right, but there's so much distortion that it's hard to distinguish them as they blend into the mix.

🔊 **Listen Up**

To the way the piano notes are cut off the third time through the intro.

To the rap fills that are panned hard right and left in the second verse.

To the bass fill at 2:23 in the third verse, proving that a bass is actually present in the recording.

To the guitar feedback that pans from right to left at the very end.

To the drum and bass accent at 1:22 of the second verse.

THE PRODUCTION

This is not a very complex song and neither are the individual parts. The drum part really stands out, as does the lead vocal, and these are usually the most important parts in any hit song. The song breathes dynamically, maintaining the listener's interest by going from quiet in the intro to loud in the verses to louder in the chorus and back again.

There are also some nice variations in the verses that make each of them a little different. At the end of bar 16 in the second verse, the drums and bass accent beats 3 and 4, and then at the beginning of bar 17 of the third verse, there is a 2-beat instrumental break; both are excellent production tricks. Interestingly, not all of the instruments end at the same time at the end of the song, but it's tough to hear, as the fade is quick. If the song were produced today, that would no doubt be fixed.

Lady Antebellum
Just a Kiss

SONG FACTS

Album: *Own the Night*
Writers: Hillary Scott, Charles Kelley, Dave Haywood, Dallas Davidson
Producer: Paul Worley
Studio: Warner Studios (Nashville)
Release Date: May 2, 2011
Length: 3:41
Sales: 2+ million
Highest Chart Position: #1 U.S. *Billboard* Country and Adult Contemporary Songs charts

"Just a Kiss" is the first single from Lady Antebellum's third album *Own the Night*. Despite the trio's country leanings, this song doesn't sound much like country music. In fact, it reached #7 on the *Billboard* Hot 100 chart; it was also #1 on the Hot Country chart, with sales of more than 2 million. "Just a Kiss" is what you might call a "power ballad" and has a lot more characteristics of a rock or pop song than a country one.

The song was quickly written in only a day by band members Hillary Scott, Charles Kelley and Dave Haywood, along with friend Dallas Davidson, and drew upon each writers' personal experiences about their previous relationships.

The album *Own the Night* went on to not only top the U.S. *Billboard* charts, but went Top five in the U.K., Australia, Canada, New Zealand and Scotland, and later won the 2012 Grammy for Best Country Album. The album also sold more than 2 million units worldwide.

THE SONG

"Just a Kiss" uses a very simple, traditional, yet effective pop form that looks like this:

intro | verse | chorus | interlude | verse | chorus | bridge | interlude | chorus | ending

The intros and interludes are very short, and the song has a real ending, which isn't that unusual these days. The lyrics actually work better in the context of the song rather than if read by themselves, where they feel somewhat clunky.

The BPM of the song is 71.

THE ARRANGEMENT

When you have a simple song form, you need a great arrangement to keep the listener from losing interest. "Just a Kiss" uses an excellently crafted arrangement that's about as good as it gets in any genre, which is one of the reasons why it's a hit.

The song begins with an intro of piano, bass and tambourine, which continues into the first verse. On the second half of the verse, the drums and dual guitars panned the left and right enter against the male vocal, which turns into two-part male/female harmony at the end.

The chorus features three-part harmony vocals with new guitars in the left and right channels. The interlude is just a reprise of the intro only with an organ way back in the mix and a hard end on beats "3 and" and 4.

The second verse is half as long as the first and features two part harmony, and new guitars playing lines and rhythm part panned left and right. This leads to a verse that ends with three-part harmony going into the second chorus, which is identical to the first except for the strings that enter halfway through.

The bridge has a guitar playing a line on the left with the strings playing a line leaning on the right, along with two- and three-part harmony vocals. A version of the intro follows but with vocals, which then leads into the final chorus, which has the strings more prominent in the mix and adds an extra 2 bars. The outro is similar to the intro except for the inclusion of the drums and vocals. The song has a hard ending with a fade, where you can hear the organ prominently.

Arrangement Elements

The Foundation: Piano, drums, bass

The Rhythm: Soft shaker adds motion throughout the entire song

The Pad: Subtle organ from the second verse onward, whole-note electric guitar strums in the chorus, synth string pad in the second and last choruses and bridge

The Lead: Lead vocals

The Fills: None really, although the string lines in the chorus can almost be thought of as fills

---

THE SOUND

The sound of "Just a Kiss" is really big and present. If you were to get picky from an engineering standpoint, you might say that the bass in the bridge is a little too big as the notes start to blur when the line gets more complicated—but it sounds great other than that. The vocals have a slight delayed reverb, but for the most part, all the elements are pretty much in your face with only slight ambiance to develop the layers. The song isn't too compressed and you certainly never hear it when it's used.

Listen Up

To the unexpected heavy accents at the end of the first interlude.

To the tambourine in the intro and first verse.

To the guitar fills on the left and right channels during the second verse.

To the strings that enter in the bridge and last chorus.

THE PRODUCTION

This is pretty much a state-of-the-art Nashville production by Paul Worley. Not only is the song layered especially well, it has a lot of little things that mostly go unnoticed in songs like this. Most notable are the harmony vocals in the last interlude and the small but effective change in the melody in the last chorus. And, of course, it's so nice to have a real ending to a song.

Maroon 5
Moves like Jagger

SONG FACTS

Album: *Hands All Over*

Writers: Adam Levine, Benny Blanco, Ammar Malik, Shellback

Producers: Adam Levine, Shellback

Studio: Mutt Lange Private Studio (Lake Geneva, Switzerland)

Release Date: June 21, 2011

Length: 3:21

Sales: 12+ million

Highest Chart Position: #1 *Billboard* Hot 100, #1 in 22 other countries

Maroon 5's "Moves like Jagger" (featuring Christina Aguilera) is a former #1 and was the first Top 10 for the band. It's the fourth single off their third studio album *Hands All Over*, and was the ninth best selling single of 2011. The song was also nominated for a Grammy for the Best Pop Duo/Group Performance.

Rolling Stones frontman Mick Jagger, who the song's main hook references, later went on *The Late Show with David Letterman* to read a top 10 list entitled, "Top Ten Things I, Mick Jagger, Have Learned After 50 Years in Rock 'n' Roll." On the list was an item that read, "You don't earn a cent when someone does a song about having moves like Jagger," which brought a great laugh from the audience. Jagger has also been mentioned in other pop songs by Ke$ha ("Tik Tok") and Cher Lloyd ("Swagger Jagger").

The Song

"Moves like Jagger" has the most basic pop form that's been used in hits for decades. It's a short pop/dance song intended for radio all the way, so it fits the form completely. It looks like this:

intro | verse | chorus | verse | chorus | bridge | chorus | chorus | outro

The song has only two chords that keep repeating, but the arrangement outlines the song's sections. The intro and outro are both shortened verses with the signature whistled line over the top.

The lyrical hook and the song's premise is great, but the lyrics themselves aren't what you'd consider clever. Any attempt at rhyme seems labored at best. You almost get the feeling that the lyrics were a much lower priority in the song than the hook.

The BPM of the song is 126.

The Arrangement

The arrangement for "Moves like Jagger" is fairly sparse, although in the chorus there's a lot more going on than it seems. The song is centered around the rhythm guitar and kick drum, but the catchy whistling signature line defines the intro, the end of the choruses, and the outro. The second verse is different from the first in that harmony vocals enter at the end of the lines during the last 8 bars, and the chorus is different from the verse in that the rest of the drum kit enters as well as a very subtle synth string sound playing the rhythm and beefing up the section.

The first 4 bars of the intro have just the signature whistle and rhythm guitar playing, but on bar 5 the kick enters along with vocal ad libs. When the verse begins and lead vocal enters, the whistle mutes, and the rhythm guitar changes tone from mellow to bright thanks to a swept filter. The whistle returns on bars 7 and 8. On the the second half of the verse, the synthesizer bass enters playing a similar rhythm to the guitar. The chorus begins with a snare fill that leads to a doubled vocal with harmony, the full drum kit and a double on the guitar.

The second verse is identical to the first verse except for a rhythmic synth noise that's added in the first half and vocal harmony and claps on the second half. The second chorus is identical to the first except for the addition of a high rhythmic synthesizer, a synth pad and some vocal ad libs.

The bridge follows the same chord pattern but changes intensity as the bass synth becomes mellow. There's synth pad in the background, the drums are stripped down to just kick, and vocal "oohs and aahs" enter along with Christina Aguilera's vocal. On the second half the drums, the original bass synth and guitar reenter, along with a harmony vocal.

The last chorus is like the previous one except for the vocal ad libs, additional percussion, and a synthesizer pad. The song ends with the intro, with the last note winding down like a vinyl record stopping.

Arrangement Elements
The Foundation: Drums, synth bass, kick drum
The Pad: Harmony background vocals in the bridge
The Rhythm: Infectious rhythm funk guitar
The Lead: Lead vocals
The Fills: Whistling signature line in the chorus and at the end of the verses, vocal fills in the choruses

THE SOUND

The sound of the record is classic dance, complete with a front-of-the-mix kick drum, synth bass, extra snappy snare drum, and a ton of compression to make it as loud and punchy as possible. Check out the rhythm guitar, which has a slowly moving filter on it that starts out bright, changes to dark, and then back to bright again in the verses—another way of keeping the interest high in the song.

◀)) Listen Up

To the ambiance sound of the vocal, which sounds like a long delay with a reverb, both timed to the track.

To the doubled harmony vocals on the choruses which are back in the mix but slightly split left and right.

To the rhythm guitar in the verse where it goes from mellow to bright thanks to a slowly moving filter.

To the claps on bars 7 and 8 of the second verse.

THE PRODUCTION

One of the best aspects of "Moves like Jagger" is the way the vocals interweave, with Adam Levine and Christina Aguilera (who's featured in the bridge) meshing very well together sound-wise. It was a brilliant move to add her vocal to the song.

"Moves like Jagger" is Top 40 dance-oriented music at its finest. It has a memorable melody, a catchy lyric, a signature lead line, great vocal performances, and an arrangement that pulls the listener in. That's pretty good production technique. That said, the song tends to feel like it was sped up, as the groove feels a bit more solid dialed back 4 or 5 BPM. If you're going to sing a song about Mick Jagger, shouldn't the song feel more R&B like The Rolling Stones do?

Foster the People

Pumped Up Kicks

SONG FACTS

Album: *Torches*

Writer: Mark Foster

Producer: Mark Foster

Studio: Mophonics (Los Angeles)

Release Date: September 14, 2010

Length: 4:11 (album), 3:28 (single)

Sales: 3+ million

Highest Chart Position: #3 U.S. *Billboard* Hot 100, #1 in five other countries

Initially offered as a free download, "Pumped Up Kicks" reached #1 on the iTunes Alternative Songs chart, but its success led to a multi-album contract with Columbia Records after it received significant airplay. The song eventually spent eight weeks at #3 on the *Billboard* Hot 100 chart, and also received a Grammy award for Best Pop/Duo Group Performance.

Writer Mark Foster wrote and recorded the song in five hours while working as a commercial jingle writer. Thinking that it was only a demo, he recorded all the parts himself, and that's the version that ended up as the hit. Foster also states that he really wasn't inspired when he sat down to write the song, but forced himself into a writing session. He wrote the song after reading about the growing issue of teenage mental illness, but also incorporated his own experiences of being bullied in school.

THE SONG

"Pumped Up Kicks" gets a lot of mileage out of one basic riff that repeats with multiple melodies over the top. However, the verse and the chorus melodies are very strong, and that's what really makes the song. The form looks like this:

intro | verse | chorus | verse | chorus | bridge | chorus | chorus | chorus

All of the song's sections are about twice as long as in most pop songs, which makes the song longer, especially the intro which is a full 38 seconds. Nevertheless, it still works even with all the repetition. The form is about as basic as you can get, but the melodies and arrangement make the song what it is.

The lyrics of "Pumped Up Kicks" paint a picture of a troubled, isolated kid with visions of homicide. There are only two verses and a chorus, but the melody and the chorus hook is strong and there's much more of a story than you get in most songs.

The BPM of the song is 126.

THE ARRANGEMENT

Considering that the song is fairly simple in form and the sections are long, the arrangement makes it go. Take the intro, for instance. It begins with a programmed drum kit, but with guitars and synths constantly fading in and out on both sides of the stereo field you have something to listen to that keeps you interested in the song.

This is one of only a few songs with just three arrangement elements, but there's no rule that says that you have to use all five.

The development of the song is interesting in that the verses are very sparse and the choruses are bigger. In the second half of the second verse and chorus, an additional guitar double (a triple actually) is added to make it bigger. The bridge is like a chorus except a clean electric chordal solo enters along with group whistling of the melody, then the chorus begins again with only the doubled guitar and no bass or drums. It's tension-release, then tension-release all the way through.

This is another song that has a hard ending, but it's performed a bit more elegantly than some others by incorporating a guitar that moves across the soundfield as it fades out.

Arrangement Elements
The Foundation: Drums, synth bass, guitar double
The Rhythm: None
The Pad: Long synth pad in the choruses
The Lead: Lead vocal in the verse, lead with harmonies in the chorus
The Fills: None

THE SOUND

There are some nice ambient layers in the song. The drum track uses a medium room sound; the lead vocal in the verse uses a bandpass filter for a telephone simulation and about a 100 ms delay. The long reverb of the chorus vocals works great contrast-wise, although the reverb itself doesn't sound that great. The vocal sound is also improved with a medium delay.

The song is interesting in that the drums aren't compressed and punchy like you'd expect in most pop or rock tunes. The mix is also heavy on the vocal and not so much on the rhythm section (which is a trait of many pop songs), but it works nonetheless.

One of the cooler aspects of "Pumped Up Kicks" is that the rather round synth bass is doubled with an electric guitar to give the line some definition. That's always a good trick and has been used in Nashville on country songs (and many Beatles songs, e.g., "While My Guitar Gently Weeps") for decades.

◀ᴼᴼ Listen Up

To how the bass is doubled by a guitar to make the line more distinct.

To the slightly delayed medium decay reverb on the chorus vocals.

To how the bass/guitar double is also doubled by a keyboard in the second half of the second verse.

To how the guitar moves from left to right during the fadeout of the song.

THE PRODUCTION

There are a number of cool things here. The garage sound of the drum kit works nicely against the rest of the mix elements. The verse vocal with the telephone filter and short delay contrasts well against the clean harmony vocals of the chorus, and the subtle electric guitars against the synths provide the tension-release and element contrast that any art requires to be popular.

The real trick in this production is making a song that's composed of basically just a verse and chorus longer while keeping it interesting. In this case, it's done with an extra long intro, choruses that repeat, adding a whistling melody, and by making the chorus into a bridge by using just one word that echoes.

Adele

Rolling in the Deep

Song Facts

Album: *21*

Writers: Adele Laurie Blue Adkins, Paul Epworth

Producer: Paul Epworth

Studio: Eastcote Studios (London)

Release Date: November 29, 2010

Length: 3:48

Sales: 8 million+

Highest Chart Position: #1 *Billboard* Hot 100 as well as 12 other countries

Adele's "Rolling in the Deep" topped the charts not only in the U.S., but in many countries around the world, selling over 8 million units in the U.S. alone. The song is from her top-selling album *21*, and is the biggest "crossover" hit in more than 25 years.

To top it off, "Rolling in the Deep" won three Grammy awards including the prestigious Record of the Year and Song of the Year.

Adele's first album, *19*, also saw much success, rising to #1 in the U.K. and #4 on the U.S. *Billboard* 200. One of the singles from the album, "Chasing Pavements," was also nominated for three Grammy awards in 2009 and won for Best Female Pop Vocalist. Adele also won a Grammy for Best New Artist that year.

"Rolling in the Deep" was composed by producer Paul Epworth and Adele in a single afternoon following Adele's breakup with her boyfriend.

THE SONG

"Rolling in the Deep" is pop music at its most basic in that it relies on a bare bones form no different to countless hit records. The form is:

verse | B section | chorus/verse | B section | chorus/bridge | verse | chorus | chorus | chorus

What makes this song so bare is that there are no intros, interludes, or outros. In fact, the song ends pretty abruptly.

The lyrics to "Rolling in the Deep" are interesting in that they don't read well without the music. The rhymes seem forced, like they were settled for instead of the result of taking more time to work on them. Yet they've obviously touched a lot of people with their tale of heartache. Sometimes authenticity beats cleverness.

The BPM of the song is 104.

THE ARRANGEMENT

Once again, this is about as formulaic as you can get. That said, take special note because it works! It's a lesson on how to arrange a song without anything extra getting in the way.

The song begins with just an eighth-note guitar part and a lead vocal, which is joined by the kick drum in the second half of the verse. In the B section, simple piano triads, bass, and the rest of the drums enter. See the development?

In the chorus, a strumming acoustic guitar and piano eighth notes push the song along, as well as the entry of background vocal answers.

The last verse and first outchorus breaks down to kick and fills (which seems to be happening in all the hits these days).

In the second verse, the low piano octaves enter on the "1 and," and handclaps on the 2 and 4. In the B section, the background vocals then enter with a counter line to add motion and make it different from the first one. In the second chorus, a third part is added to the background harmonies.

The bridge is interesting in that it's the same melody and lyrics as the chorus, but the chord changes are different, which is quite unusual.

On the first half of the last verse the song breaks down to lead vocals, kick drum, and claps, with background vocal and guitar answers. On the second half, the bass reenters, along with some piano and guitar fills.

The song then goes into another chorus but it almost acts like a second bridge. The drums and guitar drop out and only the piano is left with the addition of low note whole-note octaves. The background vocals stay the same, but the lead vocal now ad libs the melody in a lower register. The next chorus is identical to the second in arrangement, but the last chorus adds an additional low vocal line.

The song ends with a surprisingly abrupt hard ending where even the long reverb on Adele's vocal track doesn't hang over.

Arrangement Elements
The Foundation: Bass, drums
The Rhythm: Eighth-note guitar in the verse, strummed acoustic and eighth-note piano in the chorus, claps
The Pad: No true pad, but in the B section the piano playing whole-note chords is like a pad
The Lead: Lead vocal
The Fills: Background vocals, occasional clean lead guitar

THE SOUND

The final mix of "Rolling in the Deep" is not that far away from the sound of a demo. The vocal has a nicely shaped long reverb, but the eighth-note guitar is so dry that it sounds like it's played in someone's garage. The drums have a big natural ambience that works, but it isn't particularly great sounding. The lead vocal is a little on the squashed side, but the rest of the track sounds natural.

🔊 **Listen Up**
To the talking in the background on the intro before Adele begins to sing.
To the long reverb on Adele's voice during the first verse and chorus.
To the guitar fills in the third verse.

THE PRODUCTION

All the song's parts are very simple, but they're performed well. The arrangement isn't very complex as most instruments play the same eighth-note pattern, and there aren't many overdubs or counter-lines that most producers use to keep the interest level up. Sometimes the best production is knowing when to leave things alone and not be tempted to add additional elements to the song. Credit producer Paul Epworth and Adele (who both wrote the song) for following their instincts and keeping it simple.

Foo Fighters

Rope

Song Facts

Album: *Wasting Light*
Writers: Dave Grohl, Nate Mendel, Taylor Hawkins, Chris Shiflett, Pat Smear
Producer: Butch Vig
Studio: Dave Grohl's garage (Encino, California)
Release Date: March 1, 2011
Length: 4:19
Sales: 1+ million
Highest Chart Position: #1 U.S. *Billboard* Rock Songs and Alternative Songs, #1 Canadian Active Rock Charts

"Rope" by Foo Fighters was the first single from the group's *Wasting Light* album, and is a former #1 on *Billboard's* Rock Songs chart. In fact, it was the Foo's second chart topper and their first to debut at the top.

"Rope" had a long gestation period before its final completion. The song began as something band leader Dave Grohl played during sound checks while on tour in 2010. An early version was recorded, but not released until resurrected for *Wasting Light*.

The album marked a return to the world of analog, as the Foos recorded and mixed the album completely in Grohl's garage in Encino, California. Because the analog gear didn't allow for easily correcting mistakes like digital audio gear can, the band rehearsed the album for three weeks before recording began. Butch Vig, who last worked with Grohl on Nirvana's huge *Nevermind* album, was brought in to produce.

Thanks to "Rope" being released before the album, *Wasting Light* debuted at #1 in 11 countries, and earned five Grammy awards, including Best Rock Album.

THE SONG

"Rope" has a somewhat typical song form but is different thanks to an altered feel and some unusual anticipations in the verses, as well as a very interesting bridge/solo section. The form looks like this:

intro | verse | chorus | interlude | verse | chorus | bridge/solo |
chorus | half-intro | outro

The song is quite sophisticated in its development even though it seems simple on the surface—a sure sign of mature writers.

The BPM of the song is 132.

THE ARRANGEMENT

The arrangement of "Rope" is typical garage band, but in a good way. There's a lot of thrashing and energy and a certain amount of freedom in the parts, but at the same time it's a very controlled chaos. Of course, this album really was recorded in singer/guitarist Dave Grohl's garage, so maybe the group took that to heart.

One of the things that makes this song interesting is the fact that it has a couple of rhythm guitars playing tremolo parts (the intro), then both guitars banging away on a strumming rhythm guitar during the verse and choruses, instead of formulated parts like you hear on most songs. A third guitar plays the heart of the riff, then enters only at the syncopated verse turnarounds.

The bass is free-floating and creates a nice tension against the chords which is very cool, as is the drum solo in the bridge (when's the last time you heard one of those?). Interestingly, some of the cool bass lines that Nate Mendel plays are in the first verse rather than the second, where things are typically changed up to sound different or for development.

Another interesting thing is that the second verse doesn't change much from the first, so the song doesn't develop much at that point, though this isn't something you'll necessarily notice when listening to the song. Yet another interesting section is the bridge, which features a drum fill/solo in the first half, and then introduces a wah guitar solo in the second half.

The song begins with a delayed guitar on the left, then another rhythm guitar on the right playing a completely different rhythm. The rest of the band then enters with another bigger and dirtier guitar playing the signature line of the song. When the verse begins, the big guitar is muted except for turnaround spots during the verse. The verse also features octave vocals. The second half of the verse is almost like a B section, but the music doesn't change except for the reintroduction of the big guitar line while the melody changes and the octaves turn into a two-part harmony.

The chorus features big rhythm guitars spread left and right with an arpeggiated guitar in the middle and the vocal is doubled, and the second half has a lower harmony entering. The interlude that follows has the band going back to the verse chords, but with a lead guitar playing a line against it.

The second verse and chorus are the same as the first, which is rare since usually another element is introduced to have them develop and stay interesting. The first half of the bridge features a drum solo, while the second half has a guitar solo on the left channel. The next chorus is identical to the previous two.

The song then goes back to the first part of the intro with only rhythm guitar on the left, which then leads to an outro which musically is identical to the second half of the intro, only with a vocal on top. The song ends on the middle of the lead riff.

Arrangement Elements
The Foundation: Bass, drums
The Rhythm: Rhythm guitars in the verse
The Pad: Power chords in the chorus
The Lead: Lead vocal, interlude guitar, drum solo, wah solo
The Fills: Guitar on the riff turnaround

THE SOUND

Taylor Hawkins' drums have a high-class garage feel to them in that they sound great, but they also sound like they were recorded with a single stereo mic and maybe a kick drum mic (actually not the case). Notice that no one drum, especially the snare, feels separated from the other drums. That's something you rarely hear these days.

The song is pretty compressed, but it's done in such a way that you never notice it. It's also pretty much in your face ambience-wise with no long reverb tails. I'd venture to say that most of the time it's the natural ambience of the room that is heard.

◀))) **Listen Up**

To how the vocal seems pretty buried in the mix, but that only emphasizes the band more and makes it seem more powerful.

To the two rhythm guitars on the intro spread hard left and right.

To the wah solo in the bridge panned hard left.

To how the bass line changes at the end of the first half of the first verse.

THE PRODUCTION

It's the performance of all the players that really makes the song. Just as you'd expect from a band that's been together 10+ years, they're extremely tight and you can feel the energy and enthusiasm in the tracks. The interplay of the guitars in the intro and verses is great, both from an arrangement and sonic standpoint, as are the octave vocals in the verse and harmonies on the B section.

Want an example of a great rock band? It's the Foos. And Butch Vig does a great production job.

The White Stripes
Seven Nation Army

SONG FACTS

Album: *Elephant*
Writer: Jack White
Producer: Jack White
Studio: Toe Rag Studios (London)
Release Date: March 7, 2003
Length: 3:52
Sales: 5.5+ million worldwide (album)
Highest Chart Position: #76 U.S. *Billboard* Hot 100, #1 U.S. *Billboard* Modern Rock Tracks, #7 U.K. Singles Chart

"Seven Nation Army" is one of the best-known songs by The White Stripes and the lead track from their album *Elephant*, which marked their major-label debut. The song went on to become very popular in European football stadiums and with college marching bands. It also won the 2004 Grammy award for Best Rock Song and was named #23 on *NME*'s list of 150 Best Tracks of the Past 15 Years—all this from a song that the band's labels in the U.S. and U.K. didn't even want to release as a single.

The album was recorded on 8-track tape and pre-1960s recording gear, as writer/producer/guitarist Jack White refused to use a digital audio workstation at any time during the writing or recording of the album.

THE SONG

"Seven Nation Army" is all about the riff the song is built on. In fact, it's one of the few songs that has an instrumental chorus that's built on the central riff of the song. The form looks like this:

intro | verse | turnaround | chorus | intro | verse | turnaround | chorus (2X) |
intro | verse | turnaround | chorus | end

The form is a cross between a normal 16-bar pop verse and a 12-bar blues. It's 16 bars long, but there's an additional 2-bar turnaround that leads into the instrumental chorus.

The lyrics, which state the title only once, reflect how The White Stripes were dealing with their then new-found popularity. "Seven Nation Army" actually refers to what writer Jack White called the Salvation Army when he was kid. Considering that the song is based on a repeating riff, the melody is quite good in that it develops during the second half of the verse.

The BPM of the song is 120.

THE ARRANGEMENT

The arrangement for "Seven Nation Army" is simple but very effective. The song begins with the bass sound (actually a 1950s Kay 6-string acoustic/electric guitar, through a DigiTech Whammy pedal set an octave down) and is joined by the kick, floor tom, and hi-hat after 2 bars. After the riff is played two more times, the verse vocal enters; and halfway through the verse, the snare enters. During the 2-bar turnaround, a doubled, big-sounding guitar comes in and continues into the first chorus.

The second verse and turnaround are identical to the first, but the second chorus is joined by a slide guitar and is twice as long. Once again, the next intro, verse, and turnaround are identical, with the exception of some guitar feedback that hangs over into the intro. The last chorus is identical to the first, as the slide guitar is not present and it's the same length. The song has a hard ending, with an additional reprise from what sounds like a previous take.

Arrangement Elements
The Foundation: Drums and bass guitar
The Rhythm: Drums
The Pad: None
The Lead: Lead vocal in the verse, doubled electric guitar in the chorus
The Fills: None

THE SOUND

"Seven Nation Army" was recorded on 8-track analog tape in a studio where no equipment was newer than 1963, hence the vintage sound. The song has a number of interesting sonic quirks. First of all, the guitar playing the bass part is panned to the left, and if you listen closely, you can hear some "boing" from the amp's spring reverb. Then, the drums are recorded in mono, which is extremely unusual for this day and age but quite the norm back in the days when there was a maximum of only eight tracks to work with. Finally, the vocals are somewhat distorted, but that seems intentional rather than the result of some gear anomaly or poor technique.

Of course, everything is dry as a bone, and whatever is panned to the right side is more of a ghost double until the very last chord of the song.

Photo: © atlasicons.com

🔊)) **Listen Up**

To the reverb "boing" on the guitar amp during the "bass" part.

To the mono drums, with the toms and hi-hat panned to the center.

To the distorted vocals.

To how the bass and guitar lean to the left of the stereo field.

THE PRODUCTION

Jack White is a throwback to a previous time in many ways, and his production sense certainly proves that. From the concept of recording on analog and limiting the band to only eight tracks to the sparse arrangement and simple song form, "Seven Nation Army" is so retro it could well have been made in the '60s. That said, what is retro to some is cutting edge to others, and Jack White produced a hit that continues to echo around the world.

Kelly Clarkson

Since U Been Gone

SONG FACTS

Album: *Breakaway*

Writers: Max Martin, Lukasz Gottwald

Producers: Max Martin, Dr. Luke

Studio: Cosmos Studios (Stockholm, Sweden)

Release Date: November 16, 2004

Length: 3:08

Sales: 2.5+ million U.S., 12+ million worldwide (album)

Highest Chart Position: #2 U.S. *Billboard* Hot 100, #5 U.K. Singles Chart

"Since U Been Gone" was the last song recorded for Kelly Clarkson's second album, *Breakaway*. Originally intended for Pink, the song was written by Dr. Luke and producer/writer extraordinaire Max Martin. After Pink turned it down, it was then offered to Hilary Duff, who also passed. At the behest of record-label impresario Clive Davis, the song was then offered to Clarkson, who gave it a harder edge by adding heavier guitars and drums than were in the demo.

The song peaked at #2 on the U.S. *Billboard* Hot 100 and went on to win several awards, including a Grammy award for Best Female Pop Vocal Performance, the Choice Single award at the Teen Choice Awards, and the Best Pop Sing-Along Song at the 2005 XM Nation Music Awards. It also went Top 10 in much of the world and was named #482 of the 500 Greatest Songs of All Time by *Rolling Stone* magazine.

THE SONG

"Since U Been Gone" is like most Max Martin songs in that it follows a fairly common pop formula, but not without its own little twists. The song begins with a short 2-bar intro into a standard 16-bar verse. The B section is only 6 bars long, with the beginning of the chorus vocal (and the title of the song) occurring on bar 6. The chorus is then an unusual 12 bars in length. The other twist occurs in the last chorus of the song, which begins with a different lyric than the hook and has a 2-bar refrain at the end. The song ends on a 4-bar intro, with the vocal hook repeated at the beginning of what would be bar 5.

intro | verse (16 bars) | B section | chorus | verse (8 bars) | B section | chorus | bridge | interlude | chorus | chorus (plus 2 bars) | ending

The lyrics of the song don't read well, but as with all good lyrics, they fit the music. The story isn't particularly special, but it works for a pop song. The melody, however, is a different story, as it develops throughout the verses, the choruses, and especially in the bridge, where the vocals soar.

The BPM of the Song is 132.

THE ARRANGEMENT

"Since U Been Gone" isn't as dense or synthesizer-driven as other hits produced by Max Martin, but it has all the same interesting twists and turns. The song begins with an electric guitar playing eighth notes for 2 bars, and then the verse starts with the lead vocals and drums. Halfway into the verse, the bass enters along with an additional, different-sounding guitar playing in a higher register. At the B section, the vocals are doubled and a synth playing a single pedal note on beats 2 and 4 enters, while guitar feedback slowly builds in volume and is cut off at the end of bar 5.

The chorus features a doubled lead vocal on each side of the soundfield, joined by a harmony vocal. The guitars get bigger and more distorted while the rhythm section plays with more intensity.

On the second verse, the instrumentation is joined by a dark-sounding synth line on the left side, while another higher vocal is added, which rotates between singing a harmony and an octave. The title line at the end of the verse is doubled and split far left and right. The B section is the same, except that the lead vocal is joined by the wide doubled harmonies, as well as a mono harmony in the center.

The second chorus is the same as the first, except for a slight change in the melody halfway through. In the bridge, the vocal begins with the wide doubled harmonies, but returns to the lead vocal with the high octave unison part. The bridge is followed by an interlude consisting of a distorted guitar line, with drums added at the beginning of the second pattern. Fills on the bass guitar and toms accent the third and fourth times through the pattern, as guitar feedback builds.

The third chorus is the same as the previous one (except for the lead vocal answers after the main vocal lines), but then it changes completely with a new melody. In the last chorus, a new vocal ad-libs over the top of the main melody line. The song ends as it began, with the guitar, drums, and bass playing whole notes underneath the vocal. During the outro, the guitar feedback builds once again, only to be cut off where the vocal speaks by itself.

Arrangement Elements
The Foundation: Bass and drums
The Rhythm: Rhythm guitar
The Pad: None
The Lead: Lead vocals
The Fills: Synth in second verse, guitars, vocal answers

THE SOUND

"Since U Been Gone" has a lot of interesting sonic layers. In the verses, while the lead vocals and drums are dry, the guitar on the right side has a dark-sounding echo in the left channel. There's a long, timed echo on the vocal in the B section, and the doubled chorus vocals have a short reverb to give them some space as well as change the sound of the section. The answer vocals in the second verse also have a long delay that only repeats once.

The reverb on the interlude guitar is a bit trashy sounding, but it introduces a new layer to the mix. At the end of the song, it has a nice reverb to give it some space.

Though the song is pretty compressed, it still has some effective dynamics.

◀)) Listen Up

To the high octave vocal in the second verse and bridge.

To the back-and-forth guitar in the space at the beginning of the chorus.

To the delay with the single repeat on the answer vocals in the second verse.

THE PRODUCTION

When "Since U Been Gone" was released, Max Martin was already a superstar producer, but Dr. Luke was just getting his start. The team proved to be formidable, however, and managed to change the direction of Kelly Clarkson's career, as well as take her vocal performance to new heights. Even more interesting is the fact that although synth lines are found in both the second verse and the bridge, they're relatively minor parts—the song is completely guitar based, which is seldom heard in a Martin production.

Although sometimes there may be more tracks than what seems obvious, from what can be heard, the song has relatively few parts; this is a tribute to both the simplicity of the production and an arrangement that works particularly well. Combine great performances with great production, and you can see why the song was a hit.

Sheryl Crow
Soak Up the Sun

SONG FACTS

Album: *C'mon, C'mon*

Writers: Sheryl Crow, Jeff Trott

Producer: Sheryl Crow

Studio: Various studios

Release Date: March 25, 2002

Length: 4:52 (album), 3:17 (single)

Sales: 2.5+ million worldwide (album)

Highest Chart Position: #17 U.S. *Billboard* Hot 100, #1 U.S. *Billboard* Adult Top 40, #16 U.K. Singles Chart

"Soak Up the Sun" was the lead single from Sheryl Crow's 2002 album *C'mon, C'mon*, which was nominated for a Grammy award in the category of Best Rock Album in 2003. In addition, "Soak Up the Sun" was nominated for Best Female Pop Vocal Performance. The song features singer Liz Phair on background vocals.

THE SONG

"Soak Up the Sun" is one of those songs that appears to be simple on the surface, but there's more going on than meets the ear. The song form looks like this:

intro A | intro B | verse | verse | chorus | intro B | verse | B section (4 bars) | chorus | intro B | verse | B section (5 bars) | chorus | chorus | chorus

The form is unusual in that it has two intros: one that's based on loops and heard only once, and the other that features the song's main instruments and is heard multiple times. Although "Soak Up the Sun" has no bridge, there is a B section that occurs unexpectedly (instead of just another verse) at the end of the third and fourth verses, with the second B section getting an additional bar. That form change, along with the arrangement, keeps the interest high throughout the song.

The song's melody is very strong both in the verse and especially in the chorus, which contains the highly memorable and singable hook. The lyrics don't all rhyme, but they don't sound or feel forced either, as they tell a story of being down but not out.

The BPM of the song is 124.

THE ARRANGEMENT

Just like the song form, "Soak Up the Sun" has a much more complex arrangement than you might think on first listen. It has many more layers to the arrangement than do most pop songs, and these layers glue the song together.

The intro is made up of various loops over what sounds to be an old record playing. This leads into the second intro, which consists of drums and an electric-guitar riff played through a Leslie speaker in the center of the soundfield, with doubled acoustic guitars answering on each side. The glue holding the arrangement together is an organ pedaling a single note way back in the mix. While not heard clearly, it's integral to the song, as it would sound empty without it.

When the doubled vocal enters in the first verse, the Leslie guitar exits but the other instruments remain. The Leslie guitar then returns in between verses. For the chorus, the vocals are joined by the bass, doubled harmony vocals, and multiple electric guitars panned left and right; and the doubled acoustics now strum to add motion. On the second half of the chorus, a slide guitar enters to add additional motion.

When the intro returns, the instrumentation is the same as before, except the bass plays the first part of the riff and is answered by acoustic guitars along with an electric. At the end of the second verse, the first B section begins, consisting only of the lead vocal and electric guitars doubled left and right against the drums, with a muted bass guitar.

The instrumentation on the second chorus is the same as the first, except the slide guitar enters right away instead of waiting until the second half. Then on the next intro, instead of the Leslie guitar, a different electric guitar line is played. The fourth verse is different from the others, as the bass and electric guitars exit and the section is carried by the drums, acoustic guitars, and organ pad behind the doubled vocals. The next B section has the same instrumentation as the previous one, but there is an additional bar at the end.

The three outchoruses are interesting in that the instrumentation remains the same for the first two, but the melody vocals change slightly on chorus three, and background harmony and answer vocals enter on chorus four. On the final chorus, everything breaks down to acoustic and electric guitars, bass, organ pad, and vocal.

Once again, like most hit songs, the dynamics vary throughout to keep things interesting.

Arrangement Elements
The Foundation: Bass and drums
The Rhythm: Strummed acoustic and electric guitars
The Pad: Organ and distorted electric guitar
The Lead: Vocal
The Fills: Slide guitar in chorus, harmony vocals on fifth chorus (second outro chorus)

THE SOUND

Except for the vocals, "Soak Up the Sun" isn't what you'd call a clean mix, in that you don't necessarily hear each element distinctly. There are a lot of guitars, but they all pretty much blend into one another; and the organ pad is buried, but that's a good thing as it helps glue everything together.

With dry instruments and vocals, the song seems to have no effects. As a result, any layering is done mostly through level and tone. There is a fair amount of panning, with all the guitars—except for the Leslie guitar and slide—panned to one side or another to stay out of the way of the vocals.

The drums are unremarkable; the kick, sounding big and round, masks the bass guitar a bit, but the bass still has enough power that you know when it's not there.

◀)) Listen Up

To the slight melody change on the third chorus.

To the new, high background vocal that enters on the fourth verse.

To the soft organ pad in the background of the mix throughout the song.

THE PRODUCTION

As with most hits, "Soak Up the Sun" breathes dynamically, with instruments entering and exiting throughout the song and new parts subtly being introduced to keep interest high. There might not be much of a change from section to section, but there doesn't have to be a lot to hold your attention.

Sheryl Crow, who produced the song as well, has excellent production instincts, knowing what's important and what's not, and what has to breathe and what doesn't. No wonder the song still has life in commercials all over the world.

Gotye (featuring Kimbra)
Somebody That I Used to Know

SONG FACTS

Album: *Making Mirrors*
Writers: Wally De Backer, Luiz Bonfa
Producer: Wally De Backer
Studio: Gotye's parent's barn (Mornington Peninsula, Victory, Australia)
Release Date: July 5, 2011
Length: 4:05
Sales: 9+ million
Highest Chart Position: #1 U.S. *Billboard* Hot 100, #1 in 25 other countries

Gotye's "Somebody That I Used to Know" (featuring Kimbra) is one of those rare songs that hit #1 the world over. It is the second single from Gotye's third studio album *Making Mirrors*, and was a recent #1 on *Billboard's* Hot 100—a rarity for an Australian artist. It was the biggest selling single in the U.K. in 2011, topping more than a million in sales, and sold more than four million in the U.S. The song also went Top 10 in more than 30 countries, making it a bona fide international hit and Gotye (and to a lesser degree Kimbra) a worldwide star.

The song was on the *Billboard* Hot 100 chart for 15 weeks before it was performed by both the actors of Glee and two contestants of *American Idol*, and then by Gotye and Kimbra on *Saturday Night Live*, which helped it rocket to #1. Once there, it stayed at #1 for eight consecutive weeks.

"Somebody That I Used To Know" went on to win APRA awards in 2012 for Most Played Australian Song and Song of the Year, and Teen

Choice awards for Choice Rock Song and Choice Break-up Song. It also won Grammy awards for Record of the Year and Best Pop Duo/Group Performance.

THE SONG

"Somebody That I Used to Know" has an interesting song form in that it doesn't really have a bridge, yet contains another section that almost acts like one. The form looks like this:

intro | verse | interlude | verse | chorus | interlude |
verse | B section | chorus | outro

The first two verses are 16 bars each, but the third verse that Kimbra sings is 8 bars with another 8 bars that can be classified as either a B section or a bridge. Regardless of how you look at it, changing the second half of the third verse is very effective and definitely heightens the interest and raises the energy (it's an appoggiatura), which is what a bridge is supposed to do.

The lyrics of the song, while not overly clever, tell a story that most of us can relate to, but, as it turns out, is seldom written about. If you haven't noticed, common themes and phrases make hits. The melody is especially strong in the chorus, and while the hook isn't really part of the melody, it's just as effective.

The BPM of the song is 128.

THE ARRANGEMENT

On the surface this seems like a simple arrangement but it's really quite sophisticated. There's a lot going on, but you never find an instrument really playing a big wide chord as there are mostly single-note phrases, which is quite unusual in most pop records.

Listen to how the arrangement develops. It starts off sparse, gets a little bigger in the intro, backs off again during the verse, then gets large during the chorus, then back down again into the interlude, and so forth. That's the essence of a good arrangement in a pop song.

The song begins with an acoustic guitar loop, a second acoustic guitar playing a counter line, muted bells playing the intro line and what sounds like either a loosely tightened floor tom or tympani panned to the far left in the soundfield. When the verse begins, the lead vocal enters but the muted bells and the second acoustic guitar discontinue playing along with a bass that's low in the mix. The second guitar reenters halfway through the verse.

An interlude follows the verse that has the second acoustic guitar playing the same figure as during the intro, with a synth entering to play a new melody and a tom playing a new rhythm panned to the right channel.

On the second verse, the synth melody ceases playing but all the other instruments continue playing their same figures, then a guitar with a repeating delay enters on the left side playing lines against the melody. The last two bars of the verse are stripped down to only the acoustic guitar loop before the chorus begins. On the chorus, the vocal is doubled, a quarter note muted cowbell (or something that sounds like it) enters on the right side, a tuned percussion instrument enters on the left side and the intro synth enters again. The bass is also much louder in the mix.

The interlude continues with the vocal answering the intro muted bell line with the hook of the song. Halfway through, a synth with a string patch enters playing a counter line. That leads back to the first interlude again, this time with a different guitar counter line.

For the second verse with Kimbra singing, what sounds like recorder samples are played in the holes between the vocal phrases. On the second half of the verse, both the chords and the melody changes as the floor tom rhythm returns on the right side, but louder than before.

On the last chorus, Gotye again sings the melody while Kimbra sings the first set of background vocal harmonies answered by male (presumably Gotye's) background vocals. On the outro, harmony background vocals answer the lead vocal and add harmony. The song then goes back to the original intro only with a vocal over the top. The song ends on a muted bell glissando into a long reverb decay.

Arrangement Elements
The Foundation: Bass, drum (mostly tom) loops
The Rhythm: Acoustic guitar
The Pad: Background vocals during the chorus
The Lead: Lead vocals, synth lines in the intro and chorus
The Fills: Guitars in the verses, background vocals in the chorus and outro

THE SOUND

The sound of "Somebody That I Used to Know" is fairly sophisticated, with lots of effects layers. First you have the acoustic guitar that's completely dry, in contrast to every other instrument, which have some degree of ambience. Most of the synth lead lines have a long reverb which sound really good as they blend well into the track.

The vocals are also layered with both Gotye's and Kimbra's lead vocals getting a long reverb, but most of the background vocals are pretty dry. You can really hear the sound of the reverb after the hard ending to the song. Notice that the chorus lead vocals are doubled, helping to give the song a thicker more dynamic sound at that point.

There's a spot in the song where the background vocals distort a little (at around 3:10), but otherwise it sounds pretty clean. The fact the Gotye recorded "Somebody That I Used to Know" (and the album for that matter) in his parent's barn in Victoria, Australia says much of his skill as both an engineer and a producer.

🔊 **Listen Up**

To the repeating delay on the guitar fills in the second verse.

To how the guitars, percussion and mono loops play fills throughout the song and are panned to the left and right.

To the tympani and toms playing different rhythms on the far left and right of the soundfield.

THE PRODUCTION

"Somebody That I Used to Know" is an example of modern production at its best. Gotye (Wally De Backer to his friends) has a distinctive way of putting the song together in a way that's sparse with virtually no instruments playing big chords, yet it sounds big and dynamic. The loops really work without sticking out, and the background vocals on the outchorus are excellent as they weave back and forth, sometimes high, sometimes low, sometimes just Gotye, sometimes just Kimbra, sometimes both. The song's worldwide hit status is well deserved.

The Black Keys
Tighten Up

SONG FACTS

Album: *Brothers*
Writers: Dan Auerbach, Patrick Carney
Producer: Danger Mouse (Brian Joseph Burton)
Studio: The Bunker Studio (Brooklyn, NY)
Release Date: 2010
Length: 3:34
Highest Chart Position: #1 U.S. *Billboard* Rock and Alternative Charts

The Black Keys' "Tighten Up," a song from their 2010 *Brothers* album, was their first song to ever chart. It went on to hit #1 on *Billboard's* Alternative Songs and Rock Songs charts. "Tighten Up" has been used on games such as *FIFA 11* and *Rocksmith*, has been featured on a Subaru commercial, on the *Gossip Girl* television show, and the films *I Am Number Four* and *Bad Teacher*. It was also chosen by *Rolling Stone* magazine as one of the 15 best whistling songs of all time.

"Tighten Up" was the last song written for the album and came about as a result of the duo having a friendly hang out with their producer friend Danger Mouse (Brian Burton). It was the only track on the album that Burton was involved in, and according to all involved, was written with the express intent of getting on the radio. That mission was accomplished, as it went on to become the band's most widely recognized song.

The album *Brothers* went on to sell more than a million copies in the U.S. alone, and was nominated for five 2011 Grammy awards, winning

Best Alternative Music Album, while "Tighten Up" won Best Rock Performance by Duo or Group. The song was also nominated for a Best Rock Song Grammy, but did not win.

THE SONG

"Tighten Up" is an odd song, form-wise. It has an instrumental hook that acts as a chorus, and the end of the song has a different feel altogether, almost like a different song. The form looks like this:

intro | verse | interlude | verse | chorus | verse | interlude | verse | chorus | (new feel) intro | verse | chorus | end

You'd think a song that only has a vocal in the verses and only two sections that repeat would be boring, but it's not, and a lot of that has to do with arrangement. The fact that each chorus is played differently and each have different lengths, along with an odd bar or two thrown in for good measure before and after the choruses, provides a way to hold the listeners' attention.

The lyrics to "Tighten Up" are pretty "moon, June, swoon," but they work in the context of the song. This goes to show that you don't have to be a brilliant lyricist to have a hit.

The BPM of the song is 110 for the first half and 98 for the second.

THE ARRANGEMENT

Although the form of "Tighten Up" is somewhat unique, the arrangement follows a more traditional pop technique of adding instruments as the song goes along to develop the dynamics and keep the interest level high.

The song begins with a pre-intro of bass and tambourine, which leads into the intro that adds kick drum, a guitar playing on the "2 and" and "3 and," and doubled whistles. After 4 bars a new guitar line enters on the left channel. The verse has the full drum kit entering, which leads into an interlude with two guitars, a lower one in the left channel and a higher one on the right, playing a line. The next verse is identical to the first except the lower guitar on the left plays the interlude line as of bar 5.

The chorus then begins with the melody played by octave guitars on the right, with a very active rhythm guitar on the left. The next verse goes back to the stripped down version of the first, which then goes back to an interlude. Another verse begins, this time with an organ pad to make it different from the previous one.

The song then transitions to a new feel that has the drums without the snare delay, quarter notes on the rhythm guitar on the left that's doubled with a different sounding rhythm guitar on the right. There's a short intro of 4 bars where the band goes through the chord pattern once, then the verse vocal enters. For the chorus, the feel and instrumentation stays the same except for a ring modulated guitar that plays the melody line. The song ends on the last chord of the chorus, with the melody guitar resolving to the line to the one chord and fading as it modulates.

Arrangement Elements
The Foundation: Synth bass, drums
The Pad: Organ in the third verse
The Rhythm: Tambourine
The Lead: Vocal, guitar, whistle, synth
The Fills: Guitar line

THE SOUND

The sound of this song is just as interesting as its form and arrangement. The tambourine that plays through most of the song and establishes the rhythm is lightly flanged, while the drums are pretty much dry and in your face. The synth bass is all low end and doesn't come across very well on small speakers as a result, but it fits the song exactly how it sounds.

The vocals are slightly distorted on the first half of the song and have some room reverb with a very slight delay double. The guitars all lay nicely together as they each have different sounds and are panned away from each other, except for the lead guitar line which is doubled an octave higher. The guitar riff at the end of the song is modulated with a flange or resonator.

 Listen Up

To the bar of quarter-note bass added at the end of the verse just before the chorus.

To the two guitars playing the octave melody line on the right side and a guitar playing a much more active chordal figure on the left.

To the chorus effect on the tambourine.

To the delay on the snare drum on the right channel of the first part of the song.

To the second part of the song when the snare drum delay is removed and the snare is more centered between the speakers.

THE PRODUCTION

The song was produced by Danger Mouse, and he gives it a very cool marriage of high and low tech. The arrangement is a thing of brilliance, with the chorus changes, the melody line stutter, and the odd bar thrown in between verses and choruses. These types of things can make a song interesting and unique. It might not seem it on the surface, but "Tighten Up" is a great lesson in production.

The Strokes

Under Cover of Darkness

Song Facts

Album: *Angles*

Writers: J. Casablancas, A. Hammond, Jr., F. Moretti, N. Valensi

Producers: Gus Oberg, Joe Chiccarelli, The Strokes

Studio: One Way Studio (New York)

Release Date: February 11, 2011

Length: 3:56

Highest Chart Position: #12 U.S. *Billboard* Alternative Songs, #3 Canadian Rock Songs chart

The Strokes' "Under Cover of Darkness" was the first single from the band's fourth album *Angles,* which was a big hit in many parts of the world, reaching #1 in Australia and #6 in China, among other countries. Although it wasn't a huge worldwide hit, England's *NME* magazine placed the song at 133 on the list of "150 Best Tracks of the Last 15 Years."

The album was created under some band turmoil and took more than two years to complete. After starting and stopping the project a number of times, the band recorded largely without singer Julian Casablancas being present. The acrimony was such that when it was time to record his vocals, Casablancas did so at a different studio and sent his tracks to the band via email. Despite the fractured process, *Angles* was well received, as was the lead single "Under Cover of Darkness."

Angles went on to hit #1 on both *Billboard* Rock Albums and Alternative Albums charts, as well #1 on the Australian albums chart. It also went Top 10 in ten other countries.

THE SONG

"Under Cover of Darkness" appears on the surface to have a rather simple form, but it's more complex than it initially seems. The form looks like this:

intro | verse | B section | chorus | intro | verse | B section |
chorus | bridge/solo | B section | chorus | intro

One thing that makes this song interesting is that the second time all the sections are played, they're a lot shorter than the first. The last time they're played they're even shorter still, with the final intro line played only once. This works because the song would have been way too long otherwise, and the way each section changes keeps things interesting.

The lyrics don't exactly make sense unless you want to read into their meaning, but they're well-crafted and fit the song.

The BPM of the song is 100.

THE ARRANGEMENT

The arrangement of the song is pretty straight ahead. You hear the main instruments of the band with very little embellishment or extra parts. It's actually very refreshing to hear a song that doesn't suffer from tons of sweetening. What's more, the arrangement form only uses three elements instead of the typical four or five.

Except for some backing vocals in the B sections and choruses, the song gets its development and movement strictly from the playing and not from additional instruments entering the mix. One guitar plays the rhythm while the other plays rhythm and lead.

The intro begins with the bass, drums and two guitars that are spread to the left and right playing a line. The vocal joins in the verse, and the guitars play different rhythms with the one on the left acting more as a lead and the one on the right as the rhythm.

On the B section, the guitar sound on the right changes to the same sound as on the left and they're both doubled, and the lead vocal gets a lower harmony. This continues into the chorus and the feel changes, as a background vocal that acts as a pad enters.

The interlude is actually just half of the intro, which then introduces the second verse, which is actually half as long as well. The B section is identical to the first one, as is the second chorus except that the melody changes slightly and a high octave lead vocal double enters.

The bridge is actually a guitar solo that changes feels, then leads to another B section. The last chorus is the same instrumentally, but an additional vocal double is added as well as a change in the melody. The outro is actually only the first bar of the intro.

Arrangement Elements
The Foundation: Bass, drums
The Rhythm: Strumming rhythm guitar on the left channel pushes the song along
The Pad: None
The Lead: Vocal
The Fills: None

THE SOUND

All the elements of the song are very much in your face. The vocals are somewhat buried in the mix, but what that does is bring out the power of the band. This is a very old-school approach and quite the opposite of what a pop song normally requires, but it works very well here. The song seems to get bigger in the chorus, so it might be that the guitars are gently doubled, although it's hard to tell for sure—probably intentionally.

The song is wonderfully absent of any effects except during the guitar solo, which has a short reverb with its tail only on the left side to balance the panning.

 Listen Up

To the two different guitar parts on the intro, verses and interludes spread left and right.

To how low the vocal is in the mix in order to make the band seem more powerful.

To the reverb on the guitar solo that's panned to the left.

THE PRODUCTION

This song is what you'd expect from a production in 2011. The musicians aren't virtuosos, but they play well together and are very disciplined in their playing on the record. The attacks and releases are performed well so the band sounds extremely tight, the vocal is passionate and real, and even though some of the guitar parts are a bit outside the norm, they all fit together well.

Muse

Uprising

SONG FACTS

Album: *The Resistance*
Writer: Mathew Bellamy
Producers: Muse
Studio: Studio Bellini (Lake Como, Italy)
Release Date: August 3, 2009
Length: 5:03 (album), 3:35 (U.S. single edit)
Sales: 1+ million (single), 2.5+ million (album)
Highest Chart Position: #37 U.S. *Billboard* Hot 100, #1 U.S. *Billboard* Hot Alternative Songs, #9 U.K. Singles Chart

"Uprising" by Muse was the first single from the group's fifth studio album, entitled *The Resistance*. The song topped the charts in 19 countries, including *Billboard*'s Hot Alternative Songs chart for 17 weeks. It went on to become the theme song for a number of sports teams around the world and was used partially in the 2012 Summer Olympics opening ceremony.

The album was a huge hit, going to #1 all over the world and rising to #3 on the U.S. *Billboard* 200. It also won the band their first Grammy award for Best Rock Album in 2011.

THE SONG

Like most hit songs, "Uprising" shares commonalities with other hits while also having stark differences. The song consists of one long set of chord changes played over and over, but what sets it apart from other songs that do something similar is that the phrase is 16 bars long; that is far longer than normal and has the effect of making the sections seem quite contrasting. There is also a 4-bar setup that pedals on a single note and its octave before each section. The form looks like this:

setup | intro | setup | verse | setup | chorus | setup | verse | setup | chorus | setup | solo | setup | chorus | setup | intro | end

Even though the chord changes are the same for each, the intro, verse, and chorus all sound distinctive because the melodies are so different, with the intro line being played by a synthesizer, and the verse and chorus having very different vocal cadences as well. The song has no bridge, but a written solo before the last chorus and a slight change in the arrangement make it feel like it does.

The lyrics are well crafted, telling a story while having rhymes that don't seem forced, and both the verse and chorus melodies are very memorable and singable.

The BPM of the song is 130.

THE ARRANGEMENT

"Uprising" was made to be played live by a three-piece band, so even though there are a number of overdubs to beef up the sections, the arrangement never feels like it was artificially built or pieced together.

On the intro, the drums and bass begin on the pedal note for 4 bars of the setup section and then start the pattern that will follow for the rest of the song. At this point, a synth with a doubled string line plays an intro melody, augmented by handclaps doubled with tom fills.

On the first verse, the lead vocal enters while the synth and handclaps drop out. The handclaps and toms reenter on the next 4-bar setup before the chorus. On the chorus, the vocal changes to a different melody and is joined by the synth line from the intro. On the next 4-bar setup before the second verse, the drums drop out and then build with the guitar as it enters.

During the second verse, the guitar continues to play octaves, which helps develop the song and provides additional intensity. Synth flourishes enter on the 4-bar setup before the next chorus. The second chorus begins, and it is differentiated from the first by a lower doubled harmony vocal.

The song goes through another 4-bar setup and into a written guitar solo. The solo is played over the same chord pattern, only it's joined by handclaps doubled with toms that are answered by a vocal shout and a high synth line on the last 8 bars.

The vocals are doubled again on the last chorus, so they're slightly bigger as a new chordal guitar enters along with a new high synth line to build the song to a peak. The song then goes back into the intro, but it's played only halfway through and then changes to the setup section. Here, the handclaps, doubled toms, and shouts come back in, and the song ends on the last beat of the section.

Arrangement Elements
The Foundation: Drums
The Rhythm: Bass, handclaps, and toms
The Pad: Guitar on the last chorus
The Lead: Synth lines on the intro, lead vocal, lead guitar solo
The Fills: Doubled guitar and vocal

THE SOUND

The sound of "Uprising" is very British in that it contains a lot of sonic layers. Where the vocal seems dry, the synthesizers use a very long reverb, while the toms and handclaps use a long but different-sounding reverb. Additionally, the snare overdub features another, even brighter reverb. During the second verse, the guitar enters playing octaves, but it sounds fairly dry against the wet background.

The vocal is quite compressed. You can hear the compressor working, especially during the loud choruses where some sibilance occurs. The vocal part on the chorus is doubled with a long delay to distinguish it from the verse, and the low chorus harmony is doubled as well and spread slightly left and right—as are the doubled handclaps and tom overdubs. The intro synth line is also interesting in that the main synth is up the middle, while the doubled strings are in stereo and spread slightly behind it.

The bass sound is a combination of straight bass and synth pedal, so it sounds like a synth yet with more bottom. At 3:09, right before the guitar solo, the bass sound goes through a long filter sweep. Though there aren't many guitar parts, each sounds different, adding to the variety of colors in the track.

The mix itself features a really good drum sound that's augmented by an additional snare drum when the toms/handclaps come in. The cymbals aren't played much, and when they are, they're fairly low in the mix. The vocals are also mixed somewhat low, but this is a trick that many mixers employ with a rock band to keep the band powerful, since some of that power dissipates as the vocal gets louder, as in a pop mix.

◀))) **Listen Up**

To the handclaps and toms spread wide left and right.

To the addition of the long delay on the vocal during the chorus.

To the bass filter sweep at 3:09 before the guitar solo.

To the doubled vocals and extra guitar part on the last chorus.

THE PRODUCTION

"Uprising" is a model of modern production techniques, both from a sonic and arrangement standpoint. The layering of dry to wet elements makes the song feel neither dry nor wet, yet finished and polished. Because of the skilled arrangement, the same basic 20-bar chord pattern sounds not only different every time, but like entirely different sections.

As with all hits, the song has a lot of dynamics, with sections where most of the instruments drop out (like at 1:55, 3:09, and 3:35) and build back up to add intensity. The song also develops in intensity as it goes along, with each section adding something new to keep the listener's attention. It's a study in modern production techniques.

Green Day

Wake Me Up When September Ends

SONG FACTS

Album: *American Idiot*
Writers: Billy Joe Armstrong, Green Day
Producers: Rob Cavallo, Green Day
Studios: Ocean Way Recording (Hollywood, CA), Capitol Studios (Hollywood, CA)
Release Date: June 13, 2005
Length: 4:45
Sales: 1.6 million (single), 14+ million (album)
Highest Chart Position: #6 U.S. *Billboard* Hot 100, #8 U.K. Singles Chart

The fourth single from Green Day's mega-hit album *American Idiot*, "Wake Me Up When September Ends" was its second million-selling song. The album—which was #1 or in the Top 5 on charts worldwide—went on to win a slew of awards, including the 2005 Grammy award for Best Rock Album.

In 2009, *Kerrang!* magazine named the album the best of the decade, while England's *NME* named it #60 and *Rolling Stone* #22 on similar lists.

THE SONG

"Wake Me Up When September Ends" has a fairly unique song form. If you look at it globally, it contains just three verses and two intros. That form looks like this:

intro | verse | intro | verse | solo (over a half-verse) | intro | verse | refrain | refrain | end

If we look at it this way, we find that each verse is 36 bars long. The opening intro is 4 bars long, while the intro after the first verse is 6 bars long. The solo occurs over the change of chords in bars 17–24 of the verse, with an additional two bars at the end.

However, we can look at the song form in another way. If we look at the verse on a more micro level, considering each section ending with the phrase "Wake Me Up When September Ends" as a chorus, we find we have a series of small verses and choruses. Each of the above verses would then look like this:

verse | chorus | verse | chorus | B section | chorus

If we look at the entire song on this micro level, it would then look like this:

intro (4 bars) | verse | chorus | verse | chorus | B section |
chorus intro (6 bars) | verse | chorus | verse | chorus | B section |
chorus | B section/solo (2 extra bars) | intro | verse | chorus | verse |
chorus | chorus | chorus | chorus | end

The song is especially interesting because there's no true chorus and no bridge, and each verse (on a macro level) is 36 bars long.

The lyrics to the song tell of the passing of writer Billy Joe Armstrong's father and how he's still trying to come to terms with it. The cadence of the lyrics is a little clunky at times, but they're mostly well constructed, although the last verse is a repeat of the first. The melody is very strong, especially the song's hook.

The BPM of the song is 105.

THE ARRANGEMENT

The arrangement of "Wake Me Up" is what keeps this song interesting and always in motion. The song begins with a doubled acoustic guitar, which is joined by the vocal at the verse. Another lower-octave guitar is added at the chorus. On the next verse, the drums enter, playing the toms along with a tambourine that's hit on every other beat 4. In addition, there's a descending whole-note guitar line that acts as a pad. At the B section, another picking guitar enters, but very low in the mix, and it continues through the next chorus.

For the next intro, the doubled acoustic guitars play as in the first intro, but they're joined by another guitar playing a whole-note pad in the background. In bar 3, the drums come in, playing the same rhythm pattern as the guitars; then in bar 6, doubled distorted guitars join the mix.

On the next verse, the drums and acoustic guitars continue, along with distorted electric guitars, as a glockenspiel plays a descending pad line; and on the next chorus, the bass and distorted guitars enter playing eighth notes to make the chorus sound huge. On the following verse, a new set of guitars play the descending line, creating an even bigger sound, and the next chorus is identical to the previous. The same instrumentation continues through the B section.

On the next verse, the big, distorted eighth-note guitar parts drop out, but the bass remains; this helps to develop the song and distinguishes this verse from the ones that preceded it. The next chorus, though, is the same as the previous. The written guitar solo follows, over a B section with the same instrumentation as the previous chorus.

The solo is followed by another intro, which is stripped down to the doubled acoustic guitars with the glock and guitar harmonics playing a line over the top. That's followed by a verse with the same instrumentation plus drums. The next chorus features the same instrumentation as the previous ones, and the verse that follows is the same as the preceding verse, except that the bass enters.

The chorus that follows is big sounding, and that continues through the end of the song. The last B section is eliminated and, in its place, the chorus is repeated three times. The song ends on the downbeat of the next measure. During the fade over a distorted power chord, you can hear the delayed guitar harmonics that were in the background for most of the song.

Most unusually, there are no fills in this song.

Arrangement Elements

The Foundation: Bass and drums
The Rhythm: Intro guitar line, delayed guitar harmonics
The Pad: Guitar harmonics, glock, descending whole-note guitar lines
The Lead: Lead vocal, lead guitar
The Fills: None

THE SOUND

The sound of "Wake Me Up" is the epitome of modern rock. It's big and loud, and it's punchy, thanks to the drums. Take notice that the drums work on just about any size speaker, even small computer speakers.

There's some short-room reverb on the intro's lead vocal, but it blends so well into the track that you have to listen with headphones to hear it.

The acoustic guitar track is pretty noisy, which may be due to the noise from a condenser microphone or perhaps a tube preamp, but that hardly matters in the track.

The acoustic guitar is doubled and panned to the center, while the big electric guitars are doubled with identical sound and panned left and right. Once again, this works great for this song; many producers would change the tone or ambience of the double to make it sound different, but not here, where it proves to be the perfect fit.

◀))) **Listen Up**

To the tambourine playing on every other beat 4 of the second verse.

To the glockenspiel that enters at about 2:00 and plays through most of the verse that follows.

To the delayed guitar harmonics that enter with the band and can be distinctly heard during the song's fade out.

THE PRODUCTION

We can credit producer Rob Cavallo for making "Wake Me Up When September Ends" both gentle and powerful at the same time. The song is an excellent example of modern-day song dynamics that go from a whisper to a roar in an instant, with both parts proving equally entertaining.

The instrumental parts aren't all performed perfectly, but that's why they have such a great vibe. For instance, the acoustic guitar track is a little shaky in terms of its timing, especially on the single-note turnarounds. Did it hurt the song? Not a bit. Would most producers be tempted to make the track perfect? Absolutely. Congratulate Cavallo for resisting the temptation and giving Green Day such a huge hit.

Rascal Flatts

What Hurts the Most

SONG FACTS

Album: *Me and My Gang*
Writers: Jeffrey Steele, Steve Robson
Producer: Dann Huff
Studios: Sound Kitchen Studios (Nashville, TN), Masterfonics (Nashville, TN), Blackbird Studio (Nashville, TN)
Release Date: January 9, 2006
Length: 3:33
Sales: 2.28 million U.S. (single), 5+ million U.S. (album)
Highest Chart Position: #6 U.S. *Billboard* Hot 100, #1 U.S. *Billboard* Hot Country Songs, #106 U.K. Singles Chart

"What Hurts the Most," a song written by Jeffrey Steele and Steve Robson, was recorded by three other artists before the Rascal Flatts version made it to #1 on the *Billboard* country charts and #6 on the *Billboard* Hot 100 chart. The song came from the band's 2006 album, *Me and My Gang*, and was nominated for two Grammy awards.

The album logged three full weeks at #1 on the *Billboard* Hot 100 album chart and was the best-selling country album (second best-selling album overall) of 2006, going platinum (one million sales) within two weeks of its release. It was also BMI's Song of the Year in 2007.

THE SONG

"What Hurts the Most" follows the traditional hit-single form almost perfectly. It looks like this:

intro | verse | B section | chorus | interlude | verse | B section | chorus |
interlude (3 bars) | solo/bridge | chorus | tag | outro

If you were going to draw up the form for a hit record, this would be it. The difference here is that the execution is top-notch, which separates the song from others that might have the same form but never became hits.

"What Hurts the Most" has a great melody and a very catchy chorus that's well delivered both in terms of its performance and arrangement. The lyrics are crafted well, as none seem forced and all fit easily with the melody.

The BPM of the song is 136.

THE ARRANGEMENT

The song is a glowing example of the "new" country music in that it closely resembles layered pop music but with the addition of traditional country instruments like fiddle, steel guitar, and banjo. As you would expect from a big-budget act, this song has absolutely state-of-the-art arranging, which is needed for a song with such a relatively simple form.

What's especially cool is that all the sections of the song repeat but are slightly different the second and third times through. A good example is the line in the last bar of the first half of the intro, which is first played on acoustic guitar, then doubled with the fiddle the second time through. On the third pass, it's a steel-guitar fill.

Another great example is in the last chorus, where the song stops and the melody changes, and then the background vocals enter right afterward. Also, listen to how the second verse develops with the entrance of fiddle and electric guitar. Then in the second chorus, the steel and banjo enter.

The song begins with an acoustic guitar riff followed by a fiddle line, with a counter line played by the steel guitar and drums keeping the beat. The riff is played again, but now both the riff and the counter line ascend rather than descend like the first time. Finally, the riff is played a third time and is doubled by the bass. The verse enters, with the bass only playing the downbeat of the verse and then stopping.

The verse features a clean electric guitar picking a line on the left and an acoustic guitar playing the same line on the right. The bass enters on the B section, along with another electric guitar that strums a big chord on every chord change. Note that the vocal is doubled and there's a two-part harmony on the last line of each phrase.

The chorus features Rascal Flatt's signature three-part harmonies along with the addition of banjo, steel, and fiddle. At the end of the first chorus, the intro enters again; this time, it's half as long and the fiddle doubles the acoustic guitar riff along with the bass.

On the second verse, the bass continues to play, unlike in the first verse. There are also two additional electric guitars that enter on both the left and right sides, playing new fill lines to add motion. At the B section, the steel and fiddle enter, as does an electric lead guitar, playing a fill on the left side. There's also a background vocal answer line that's very subtle and occurs only once.

The second chorus is identical to the first, except there's a background vocal answer halfway through. The bridge begins with a 3-bar interlude that leads to a written, 8-bar guitar solo. The solo is played against a different chord pattern and lead vocal ad-libs.

The last chorus enters, builds to a peak, and then stops as the vocal melody changes and a guitar plays an upward glissando. The lead vocal varies from the parts that don't have harmonies, as the band plays with more intensity and activity to build the song to a crescendo. The last 4 bars of the chorus are repeated, with a background vocal answer as the band lies out. The outro is identical to the intro, except the opening line is played twice and ends on the final chord.

Arrangement Elements

The Foundation: Bass and drums

The Rhythm: Acoustic guitar in the verses, banjo and shaker in the choruses

The Pad: Steel guitar, big electric guitar chords during the chorus

The Lead: Fiddle in the intro and interlude, lead vocal in the verses and choruses, lead guitar in the solo

The Fills: Steel guitar answer in the interlude, background vocal answers in the last chorus

---

THE SOUND

The sound of this record is generally great. It's very clean, but it's also a bit heavily compressed, which has become the norm in modern country music. There's very little ambience that sticks out anywhere, so everything is very in-your-face, and this works well for the song.

Because many things are happening on each side of the soundfield, with different instruments entering or exiting, there's always a sense of forward motion just from the panning. What is a bit unusual is that the bass is very loud and takes up a lot of space in the mix, very much like mixes from the 1960s, when the bass was the predominant instrument of the rhythm section.

🔊 **Listen Up**

To the two electric guitars on either side, playing different lines during the second verse.

To the banjo that enters on the right side during the chorus.

To the lead guitar fill on the left side at the second B section.

To the answer harmony vocals that appear only on the last chorus at 2:45.

To the last chord of the song with a guitar on either side, and steel guitar and fiddle.

THE PRODUCTION

Everything on this recording is well executed, but Gary LeVox's lead vocal pushes the song to another level, especially on the last chorus where the melody changes over the stops. What also stands out is the drum groove, most notably the snare, which is played very behind the beat and sounds almost like a blues record. The production is all very state-of-the-art, and this is what we've become accustomed to on today's country records by major artists.

GLOSSARY

4 on the floor A drum pattern where the bass drum plays on every beat in a measure.

A-side The primary side of a 7-inch vinyl record.

B-side The secondary side of a 7-inch vinyl record.

Airplay When a song gets played on the radio.

Ambience The background noise of an environment.

Arpeggiated The notes of a chord played in quick succession.

Arrangement The way the instruments are combined in a song.

Articulation The way a note or phrase is played or sung.

Attenuator A piece of equipment that causes a decrease in level.

Automation A system that memorizes, then plays back the position of all faders and mutes on a mixing console.

Autotune A hardware device or plug-in used to adjust the pitch of a vocalist.

B section See Pre-chorus.

Bandwidth The number of frequencies that a device will pass before the signal degrades. A human can supposedly hear from 20 Hz to 20 kHz so the bandwidth of the human ear is 20 Hz to 20 kHz.

Basics See Basic tracks.

Basic tracks Recording the rhythm section for a record, which may include all the instruments of the band, but may be only the drums, depending on the project.

Bleed Acoustic spill from a sound source other than the one intended for pickup.

Bottom Bass frequencies, the lower end of the audio spectrum. See also Low end.

Bottom end See Bottom.

BPM Beats per minute. The measure of tempo.

Breakdown When an arrangement is stripped down to only one or two elements.

Bridge An interlude that connects two parts of a song, building a harmonic connection between those parts.

Build Usually a one- or two-bar section of a song where the volume builds from soft to loud.

Cadence The number of syllables in a line.

Channel In a stereo mix, the audio sent to each speaker represents a channel. There are also mix delivery formats with four, five or more channels.

Chord When two or more notes are played at once. Songs usually contain a repeating sequence of various chords called a chord progression or pattern.

Chorus (in a song) The refrain of the song following each verse, which usually contains the hook.

Chorus (electronic effect) A type of signal processor where a detuned copy is mixed with the original signal, which creates a fatter sound.

Chucks On a guitar, 8th- or 16th-note chords muted with the hand so they have a very short sustain.

Clean A signal with no distortion.

Click A metronome feed to the headphones to help the musicians play at the correct tempo.

Clip To overload and cause distortion.

Clipping When an audio signal begins to distort because a circuit in the signal path is overloaded, the top of the waveform becomes "clipped" off and begins to look square instead of rounded. This usually results in some type of distortion, which can be either soft and barely noticeable, or horribly crunchy sounding.

Competitive level A mix level that is as loud as your competitor's mix.

Compressor A signal processing device used to compress audio dynamics.

DAW Digital audio workstation. The software application and hardware that allows your computer to record and edit audio.

dB Decibel, is a unit of measurement of sound level or loudness.

Decay The time it takes for a signal to fall below audibility.

Delay A type of signal processor that produces distinct repeats (echoes) of a signal.

Direct To "go direct" means to bypass a microphone and connect the guitar, bass, or keyboard directly into a recording device.

Double To play or sing a track a second time. The inconsistencies between both tracks when played back simultaneously make the part sound bigger.

Dynamics Whether an instrument or song is played softly or loudly. Songs that vary in dynamics are found to be expressive and interesting.

Edgy A sound with an abundance of mid-range frequencies.

Effect When a sound is changed or enhanced with delay, ambience or modulation.

Element A component or ingredient of the mix.

EQ Equalizer, or to adjust the equalizers (tone controls) to affect the timbral balance of a sound.

Equalizer A tone control that can vary in sophistication from very simple to very complex. See also Parametric equalizer.

Equalization Adjustment of the frequency spectrum to even out or alter tonal imbalances.

Feel The groove of a song and how it feels to play or listen to.

Fill A short musical passage to sustain the listener's attention between melody phrases.

Flanging The process of mixing a copy of the signal back with itself, but gradually and randomly slowing the copy down to cause the sound to "whoosh" as if it were in a wind tunnel. This was originally done by holding a finger against a tape flange (the metal part that holds the tape on the reel), hence the name.

Footballs Whole notes. Long sustaining distorted guitar chords.

Four on the floor See "4 on the floor"

Groove The pulse of the song and how the instruments dynamically breathe with it. Or, the part of a vinyl record that contains the mechanical information that is transferred to electronic info by the stylus.

Guide vocal See "scratch vocal."

Hard ending An ending to a song where the music stops completely.

Harmony When a part in a song is played (or sung) by multiple instruments, each playing a different, yet related pitch, which usually sounds pleasant to the ear.

Hz An abbreviation for Hertz, the measurement of audio frequency. 1 Hz is equivalent to one cycle of a sound waveform per second. The higher the frequency of the signal, the higher the number of Hertz, and the higher the sound. Low numbers of Hertz represent low sounds.

High end The high frequency response of a device.

Hook A catchy phrase either played or sung.

Hypercompression A condition where too much compression is used and as a result leaves the song with no dynamics, making it sound lifeless.

Intonation The accuracy of tuning anywhere along the neck of a stringed instrument like a guitar or bass. Also applies to brass, woodwinds, and piano.

Iso booth Isolation booth. An isolated section of the studio designed to eliminate leakage from coming in to the booth or leaking out.

Intonation The accuracy of tuning anywhere along the neck of a stringed instrument like a guitar or bass. Also applies to brass, woodwinds, and piano.

Key When music conforms to one particular scale. If a key changes, the music then uses another scale than the original one.

kHz Kilohertz; 1 kHz = 1000 Hz.

Layered mix When the different mix elements are put into different artificial environments by using effects such as reverb and delay.

Lazy fill A drum fill that wavers behind the beat.

Leakage Sound from a distant instrument "bleeding" into a mic pointed at another instrument. Acoustic spill from a sound source other than the one intended for pickup.

Leslie A speaker cabinet primarily used with organs that features rotating speakers.

Limiter A signal-processing device used to constrict or reduce audio dynamics, reducing the loudest peaks in volume.

Loop A small audio file, usually only four or eight beats (or measures) that's edited in a way so that it can seamlessly repeat.

Low end The lower end of the audio spectrum, or bass frequencies usually below 200 Hz.

Master A final version of a recording that is destined for distribution.

Mastering The process of turning a collection of songs into a record by making them sound like they belong together in tone, volume, and timing (spacing between songs).

Mellotron A keyboard popular in the 1960s that used tapes of recorded orchestral instruments to generate its sounds.

Mid-range Middle frequencies starting from around 250 Hz up to 4000 Hz.

Mix The final balance of a recording where the individual instruments and vocals are balanced, tonally enhanced, dynamically controlled, and effects may be added.

Modulation (effect) Using a second signal to modify the first. A chorus uses a very low frequency signal to modulate the audio signal and produce the effect.

Modulation (in a song) When a song changes to a different key.

Mono Short for monaural, or single audio playback channel.

Monaural A mix that contains a single channel and usually comes from only a one speaker.

Mute To turn an instrument or voice off in a mix.

Outboard effect Hardware devices such as compressors, reverbs, and effects boxes that are not built into a console and usually reside in an equipment rack in the control room.

Outchorus A repeating chorus at the end of a song.

Out of phase The polarity of two channels (it could be the left and right channel of a stereo program) are reversed, thereby causing the center of the program (such as the vocal) to diminish in level.

Outro The section of a song after the last chorus until the end of the song.

Overdub To record along with previously recorded tracks.

Overtone The part of a sound that give it its character and uniqueness.

Pad A long sustaining note or chord.

Pan Short for panorama; indicates the left and right position of an instrument within the stereo spectrum.

Panning Moving a sound across the stereo spectrum. If a sound appears to be coming from the right or left, the majority of the volume is panned to that channel. When a sound appears to be coming from the middle, it is panned to the center, or equally to each channel.

Pedal A sustained tone.

Phase cancellation The process during which some frequencies (usually those below 100 Hz) are slowed down ever-so slightly as they pass through a device. This is usually exaggerated by excessive use of equalization and is highly undesirable.

Pitch A musical tone.

Plug-in An add-on to a computer application that adds functionality to it. EQ, modulation, and reverb are examples of DAW plug-ins.

Pocket In the "groove" (the rhythm) with the song.

Power chords Long sustaining distorted guitar chords.

Pre-chorus A section of a song between verse and chorus sections. Sometimes called a B-section. Not found in every song.

Pre-delay The time between the dry sound and the onset of reverberation. The correct setting of the pre-delay parameter can make a difference in the clarity of the mix.

Pre-production A process of familiarizing an ensemble with the songs and arrangements before recording them.

Presence Accentuated upper mid-range frequencies (anywhere from 5 kHz to 10 kHz).

Producer The musical equivalent of a movie director, the producer has the ability to craft the songs of an artist or band technically, sonically, and musically.

Production The process of overseeing and molding the sound, the arrangement, the song form, and lyrics to create the final song.

Pumping When the level of a mix increases, then decreases noticeably. Pumping is caused by the improper setting of the attack and release times on a compressor.

Punchy A description for a quality of sound that infers good reproduction of dynamics with a strong impact. The term sometimes means emphasis in the 200 Hz and 5 kHz areas.

Record A generic term for the distribution medium of a recording. Regardless of whether it's a CD, vinyl, or a digital file, it is still known as a record.

Rehearsal A practice or trial band performance.

Release The end of a sound or phrase. See also Tension and release.

Remaster To enhance the sound quality of an existing recording.

Reverb The hardware unit or plug-in that produces artificial reverberation or room ambience.

Reverberation The persistence of sound in an environment that lingers after the original sound is produced.

Rhythm section The instruments in a band that give the song its pulse, usually the bass and drums.

Roll off To attenuate either end of the frequency spectrum.

Rushed fill A drum fill that's played ahead of the beat.

Scratch vocal A temporary vocal recorded during basic tracking with the intention of replacing it later (sometimes known as a "guide vocal").

Sibilant When a vocalist singing or pronouncing a syllable that creates a "sss" or "shhh" sound that is audibly louder than other syllables.

Snare A thin drum with springs or "strainers" underneath that create a "rattling" sound.

Snare strainers The string of springs on the bottom of the snare drum.

Song form The order in which the different sections of a song are arranged.

Soundfield The direct listening area.

Stereo When a recording is mixed as two separate channels to be played through two separate speakers (right and left).

Sympathetic vibrations Vibrations, buzzes, and rattles that occur in other drums or instruments than the one that was struck.

Tempo The rate of speed that a song is played.

Tension and release Building a listener's expectations and then relaxing them, such as dissonance to harmony, or loud to soft.

Timbre Tonal color.

Timed delay A delay where the repeats are timed to pulse along with the pulse of the song.

Top end See High end.

Track A term sometimes used to mean a song. In recording, a separate musical performance that is recorded.

Transient A very short duration signal.

Tremolo A cyclic variation in volume.

Turnaround A short transition part, usually at the end of song sections such as between a verse and chorus.

Vibe The emotional atmosphere communicated to and felt by others.

Vibrato A cyclic variation in tone.

Vocoder A type of synthesizer that uses the human voice as an oscillator.

Voicing The way the notes of a chord are distributed.

BOBBY OWSINSKI BIBLIOGRAPHY

The Mixing Engineer's Handbook 2nd edition (Thomson Course Technology)
The premier book on audio mixing techniques provides all the information needed to take your mixing skills to the next level. Includes advice from some of the world's best mixing engineers.

The Recording Engineer's Handbook 2nd Edition (Course Technology PTR)
This book reveals the microphone and recording techniques used by some of the most renowned recording engineers, including everything you need to know to lay down great tracks in any recording situation, in any musical genre, and in any studio.

The Audio Mastering Handbook 2nd Edition (Course Technology PTR)
Everything you always wanted to know about mastering, from doing it yourself to using a major facility, utilizing insights from some of the world's top mastering engineers.

The Drum Recording Handbook with DVD (with Dennis Moody) (Hal Leonard)
Uncovers the secret of amazing drum recordings in your recording, even with the most inexpensive gear. It's all in the technique, and this book & DVD will show you how.

How To Make Your Band Sound Great with DVD (Hal Leonard)
This band improvement book and DVD shows your band how to play to its fullest potential: how to be tight, more dynamic, and how to improve your live show and recordings.

The Studio Musician's Handbook with DVD (with Paul ILL) (Hal Leonard)
Everything you wanted to know about the world of the studio musician including how you become a studio musician, who hires you, how much you get paid, what kind of skills you need, what gear you must have, the proper session etiquette required to make a session run smoothly, and how to apply these skills in every type of recording session.

Music 3.0 - A Survival Guide To Making Music In The Internet Age 2nd Edition (Hal Leonard)
The paradigm has shifted and everything you knew about the music business has completely changed. Who are the new players in the music business? Why are traditional record labels, television, and radio no longer factors in an artist's success? How do you market and distribute your music in the new music world—and how do you make money? This book answers these questions and more in its comprehensive look at the new music business.

Bibliography

The Music Producer's Handbook with DVD (Hal Leonard)
Reveals the secrets to becoming a music producer and producing just about any kind of project in any genre of music. The book also covers the true mechanics of production, from analyzing and fixing the format of a song to troubleshooting a song when it just doesn't sound right, to getting the best performance and sound out of the band and vocalist.

The Musician's Video Handbook with DVD (Hal Leonard)
A musician's guide to making any of the various types of videos now required by a musical artist for promotion or final product. The book explains tricks and tips used by the pros to make their videos look professional, which you can do with inexpensive gear and not much of a budget.

Mixing And Mastering With IK Multimedia T-RackS: The Official Guide (Course Technology PTR)
Learn how to harness the potential of T-RackS and learn the tips and tricks of using T-RackS processor modules to help bring your mixes to life, then master them so they're competitive with any major label release.

The Touring Musician's Handbook with DVD (Hal Leonard)
This handbook covers all you need to know as a touring musician, whether you're a sideman, solo performer, or member of a band. As a bonus, individual touring guides for guitarists, bassists, drummers, vocalists, keyboard players, horn players, and string players as well as interviews with famous and influential touring musicians are included.

The Ultimate Guitar Tone Handbook with DVD (with Rich Tozolli) (Alfred Music)
The Ultimate Guitar Tone Handbook is the definitive book for discovering that great guitar sound and making sure it records well. The book definitively outlines all the factors that make electric and acoustic guitars, and amplifiers and speaker cabinets sound the way they do, as well as the classic and modern recording and production techniques that capture great tone. *The Ultimate Guitar Tone Handbook* also features a series of interviews with expert players, technicians, recording engineers, producers and manufacturers that gives you an inside look into the business of guitar tone, and an accompanying DVD provides both an audio and visual reference point for achieving the classic sounds you hear on records.

The Studio Builder's Handbook with DVD (with Dennis Moody) (Alfred Music)
No matter how good your recording gear is, chances are you're not getting the best possible sound because of the deficiencies of your room. While you might think that it costs thousands of dollars and the services of an acoustic designer to improve your studio, the *Studio Builder's Handbook* will strip away the mystery of what makes a

great-sounding studio and show how you can make a huge difference in your room for as little as $150.

Audio Mixing Boot Camp: Hands-on Basic Training for Musicians (Alfred Music)
If you're creating your first mix and don't know where to begin, or your mixes aren't as good as you'd like them to be, this book is here to help. It features a series of hands-on mixing exercises designed to show you how to listen and work like a pro, and reveals the tips, tricks, and secrets to all the different facets of mixing, including instrument and vocal balance, panning, compression, EQ, reverb, delay, and making your mix as interesting as possible.

Audio Recording Basic Training: Hands-on Survival Manual for Musicians (Alfred Music)
A beginners' guide to producing great recordings. The book features a series of hands-on recording exercises designed to show you how to listen and work like a recording pro, and reveals the tips, tricks and secrets to all the different facets of recording, including miking a drum kit, recording vocals, and miking electric and acoustic instruments.

Abbey Road To Ziggy Stardust (with Ken Scott) (Alfred Music)
The memoir of legendary producer/engineer Ken Scott, who holds a unique place in music history as one of only five engineers to have recorded the Beatles and was producer and/or engineer on six David Bowie records (among his many other credits). In this funny, poignant, and honest account, Ken pulls no punches, telling it as he saw it.

BOBBY OWSINSKI LYNDA.COM VIDEO COURSES

Audio Mixing Boot Camp. Almost nine hours of movies outlining the various steps, tips, and tricks of mixing like the pros.

Audio Recording Techniques. A five-and-a-half-hour course that describes how to record crisp, rich vocals and instrument tracks and covers the process of miking and tracking a complete song using A-list session musicians in a top-of-the-line studio.

Mastering for iTunes. A short video that demonstrates best practices for mastering music and audio destined for sale on Apple iTunes with its new Mastered for iTunes high-resolution audio program.

Audio Mastering Techniques. A two-hour video that explores essential mastering concepts and techniques used by experienced audio engineers to create a cohesive album from a set of mixed tracks.

Also Available From Bobby Owsinski

Delay Genie iPhone App: Time your delays and reverbs to the track with this free, easy-to-use app that also has a live mode for delaying speakers or delay towers.

Bobby Owsinski's Social Media Connections

Bobby's Music Production Blog: bobbyowsinski.blogspot.com

Bobby's Music Industry Blog: music3point0.blogspot.com

Bobby on Facebook: facebook.com/bobby.owsinski

Bobby on YouTube: youtube.com/polymedia

Bobby on LinkedIn: linkedin.com/in/bobbyo

Bobby on Twitter: @bobbyowsinski

About Bobby Owsinski

A long-time music industry veteran, Bobby Owsinski started his career as a guitar and keyboard player, songwriter, and arranger, eventually becoming an in-demand producer/engineer working not only with a variety of recording artists, but on commercials, television, and motion pictures as well. He was one of the first to delve into surround sound music mixing, and has worked on more than 100 surround projects and DVD productions for a variety of superstar acts.

By combining his music and reording experience with an accessible writing style, Bobby has become one of the best-selling authors in the music recording industry. His 18 books are staples in audio recording, music, and music business programs in colleges around the world.

Bobby is a frequent speaker at universities and industry conferences the world over, he has served as the longtime producer of the annual Surround Music Awards, and he is one of the creators and executive producers for the Guitar Universe and *Desert Island Music* television programs.

Bobby's blogs are some of the most influential and widely read in the music business. Visit Bobby's production blog at bobbyowsinski.blogspot.com, his Music 3.0 music industry blog at music3point0.blogspot.com, his postings at Forbes at forbes.com/sites/bobbyowsinski/, and his website at bobbyowsinski.com.